Some day the silver cord will break,
And I no more as now shall sing;
But, O the joy when I shall wake
Within the presence of the King!

And I shall see Him face to face,
And tell the story, saved by grace:
And I shall see Him face to face,
And tell the story, saved by grace.

–SOME DAY THE SILVER CORD WILL BREAK

Roadmap Through Revelation

Published by DayStar Publishing

P.O. Box 464
Miamitown, Ohio 45041

daystarpublishing.org

Also available at truthandsong.com

Second Edition, 2013

ISBN: 9781890120757

LOCN: 2010941287

Cover and charts were created by Second Mile Media.
secondmilemedia.org/

ROADMAP THROUGH REVELATION

BY RICK SCHWORER

Dedicated to my father, Richard Lee Schworer.

"For thou hast delivered my soul from death: wilt not thou deliver my feet from falling, that I may walk before God in the light of the living?"

Psalm 56:13

This was his favorite Bible verse.

INTRODUCTION

A Personal Testimony and the Purpose of this Book

I remember when I first decided to study Revelation. I was eighteen at the time and my parents were running a missionary guest house in Papua New Guinea. This had opened up several opportunities, one of the most memorable being to teach and preach the Bible in public high schools as well as in churches from time to time.

I had the desire to do a sermon from Revelation, and so I sat down and read it in entirety one afternoon. I had heard bits and pieces of teaching about it and when I read it all the way through I couldn't help but get confused about a few things. Not the least of which was that fact that it seemed like Armageddon kept happening over and over again.

I used to think that the story of the Second Advent started at the beginning of Revelation and ended at the end of Revelation. What I mean is that I always assumed it to be chronological from beginning to end. What I learned is that if you look closer you'll see that the story of Christ's Second Coming is told four times within the book of Revelation.

I sat there very confused, wondering why there were multiple apocalyptic battles and why Christ showed up at them more than once. Then an idea came to my mind. I thought, *"I should go ask someone older than me about this!"* I know, I know, many of you are shocked that an eighteen year old would actually think of something like that. Regardless, the wise missionary that I asked about this told me something that would begin a long journey of study into Revelation.

He said something to the effect of, *"Well, you know how there are four accounts of Christ's first appearance on Earth – Matthew, Mark, Luke, and John? Same thing with his Second Coming, only all four of them are in Revelation."*

Immediately, a previously sad and dim light bulb was illuminated in a thought cloud above my head. I unloaded a flurry of questions upon him. I think that's when his eyes glazed over and he wished he had just originally said, *"Beats me, kid."*

When I discovered that Revelation is divided up four times, I tried to find a harmony of it. By that I mean a book or commentary that takes all the accounts and examines them separately and then intertwines them. There are several harmonies of the Gospels available, so I thought I could find a harmony of Revelation. I couldn't, and I still haven't. There are several commentaries that touch on the subject, but to the best of my knowledge there are no harmonies of Revelation. That's where this book comes in: it's the book I looked for when I was eighteen, only thirteen years later.

There are three purposes of this book. **The first is to be a harmony of Revelation.** To understand the end times you must understand Revelation, and the best way to study it is to examine it in accordance with the four separate accounts.

Secondly, it is to be an easy to read commentary. My desire is that you will find this to be more than a reference book that sits on your shelf and gets pulled out for a tough verse or passage. In trying to make this a book that you will read in its entirety, I have decided not to go verse-by-verse. There are several other good verse-by-verse commentaries already out on the market. This is more of an event-to-event commentary in order to keep things moving. Also, to help bring Revelation to life, there are ministories interjected periodically that tie in to what is being studied.

Thirdly, to examine all of the major Second Coming events that may or may not be in Revelation. The format of this book is based in Revelation, but it is not limited to just that book of the Bible. Events such as the Judgment Seat of Christ, the Judgment of the Nations, Ezekiel 38 and 39 and appropriate passages in Daniel will also be examined.

Lastly, before I end this introduction I want to touch on some tendencies people have when it comes to commentaries. People tend to throw the baby out with the bathwater. If they find one thing they disagree with, the book is useless to them.

I wrote this book so it could be *used*. I would never presume to write a book so it could be *believed*. What I mean by that is there is only one book that should ever be believed, and that is the Authorized King James Bible.

I hate to admit it, but I'm sure this book isn't perfect. It certainly isn't inspired, and because of that you shouldn't believe it. You should use it. Examine what I say for yourself. When it comes to end-time events, it's very difficult to be absolutely right about every detail. I'm going to step on a limb on a few things and I hope you have grace with me. I certainly believe everything I wrote here but if there is something you don't agree with take what you can and throw the rest out.

What I'm getting at is *perspective*. If you read a book with the proper perspective you can get something out of it. I read and studied many books while I was writing this one, and I can tell you that they didn't all agree on the *"finer points"* of doctrine. I was still able to get something out of them – because I used them; I didn't believe them.

I hope you can use this book to better help you understand Revelation. One of the reasons I didn't put every verse of Revelation in this book is because I hope that while you read this you will have the Bible, the book you're supposed to believe, right there next to you.

TABLE OF CONTENTS

CHAPTER ONE

THE FOUR ROADS
IN REVELATION

"Study to shew thyself approved unto
God, a workman that needeth not to
be ashamed, rightly dividing the word
of truth."

II Timothy 2:15

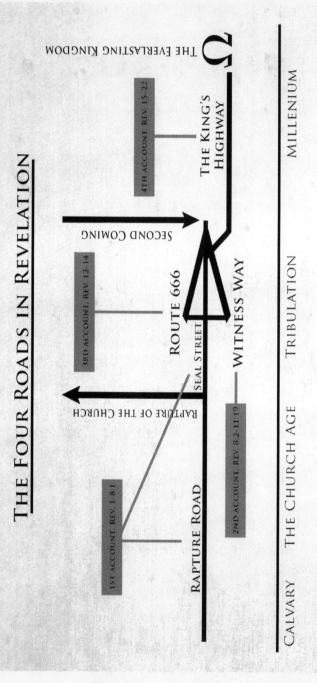

THE FOUR ROADS IN REVELATION

THE EVERLASTING KINGDOM

Ω

THE KING'S HIGHWAY

4TH ACCOUNT. REV. 15-22

SECOND COMING

3RD ACCOUNT. REV. 12-14

ROUTE 666

WITNESS WAY

SEAL STREET

RAPTURE OF THE CHURCH

2ND ACCOUNT. REV. 8:2-11:19

RAPTURE ROAD

1ST ACCOUNT. REV. 1-8:1

CALVARY   THE CHURCH AGE   TRIBULATION   MILLENIUM

I. Pitfalls

Revelation can be an intimidating book, for a lot of reasons, not the least of which is that people don't like the idea that it could be true. While several people feel that way about the whole Bible, many professing Christians try to soften Revelation, as they do many other tough places in the Bible. This pitfall is known as the **Allegorical view.**

In other words, they don't take what it says literally. They believe that the whole book is symbolic of something that really isn't nearly as scary as seven years of Hell on Earth. While it might be popular to find a way to dismiss the unpleasant parts of Revelation, one would certainly hope the exciting parts about New Jerusalem, casting crowns at His feet, and real peace on Earth are not symbolic or allegories of something far less spectacular.

Some say the book of Revelation was fulfilled back when Jerusalem was destroyed in 70 A.D., which oddly enough was before Revelation was written. This is called the **Preterist view.** John said the things in Revelation were things to come and despite the insistence of our fellow Preterist brethren there is no solid internal or external evidence that Revelation was written before the destruction of Jerusalem. Preterists ultra-literalize verses such as Rev. 1:3 and then stand the rest of the book on its head. While trying to cram the two-thousand year church age into the one-thousand year Millennium they fail to recognize the difference between it and the New Heavens and New

Earth. Suffice it to say, there are many problems with Preterism.

Closely related to the Preterist view is the **Historical view**, or the teaching that the events in Revelation have already occurred in several places in history, except for maybe the judgments. The idea is that these things in Revelation already happened under the Caesars of Rome, or maybe even Hitler. The problem is, Christ said that the Tribulation period will be so cataclysmic that we've never seen anything like it before and we'll never see anything like it again (Matt. 24:21).

The easiest way for us to be assured that Revelation should be read from the **Futurist viewpoint** is to look at how prophecy works in the Bible. When the children of Israel were prophesied to come out of Egypt, was it symbolic or did they actually come out? How about the prophecies of Christ? Isaiah 53, Psalm 22... they all happened literally – and the ones that didn't *will.*

So based upon past history, whenever there is a prophecy in the Bible we should first of all look for it to be fulfilled as literally as possible before getting any other idas.

The book of Revelation is one of the most hated, loved, and feared books of the Bible. It tells the future of the Earth and mankind in striking detail, as well as the glorious reign of the Lord Jesus Christ. It is the only book in the Bible that has a specific promise to bless the reader for just reading it (Rev. 1:3).

II. A Harmony of Revelation

A serious student of the Bible understands that you must rightly divide it. This isn't something that is optional, it is the specific prescribed manner in which God told us to study His word.

II Tim. 2:15, "Study to shew thyself approved unto God, a workman that needeth not to be ashamed, <u>rightly dividing the word of truth</u>."

By rightly dividing the Bible, we understand that many things that God told one group of people may or may not apply to us doctrinally. One of the clearest examples of this is the dietary laws given to the nation of Israel in the Old Testament (Deut. 14) and how they are rescinded in Acts 10.

There is also a very clear example of rightly dividing within a single New Testament book in the book of Matthew. In Matthew 10:5 Jesus specifically tells his apostles to avoid witnessing to the Gentiles. Then in Matthew 28:19 He tells His followers to bring the gospel unto all nations.

Consider this: is it an unscriptural idea that eating pork is a sin? The answer is no because it's right there in the Bible. However by reading Acts 10 we see that it is something that is not to be applied to us today. Is the idea that the gospel is supposed to only go to the Jews an unscriptural idea? It would be a mistake to misapply Matthew 10:5 to us today when it wasn't meant for us and when Matthew 28:19 is more appropriae.

God's method of Bible study is division. When Jesus came to this Earth the first time God had four men write four separate accounts of it. A great way to study the first coming of Christ is to use what is commonly called a "Harmony of the Gospels". A harmony is a book that will examine the four separate gospels and then pull together the identical events and place them all in chronological order.

Matthew focuses on Christ as king and Mark focuses on Christ as a servant. Luke focuses on the Lord being human, the Son of man. John is written that ye might believe, showing Jesus as the Son of God.

Just as there are four accounts of Christ's First Coming, there are also four accounts of His Second Coming and they are all contained within the book of Revelation. *This book is a harmony of Revelation.* It is a common misconception that the story of the Second Coming begins at Revelation 1:1 and goes through the entire book to the very end continuously. Not all of the accounts start at the same place and they don't all talk about the same events, but they all very clearly show the Battle of Armageddon.

The most obvious one is Christ's return in Revelation 19:

Revelation 19:11-13, "And <u>I saw heaven opened,</u> and behold a white horse; and he that sat upon him was called Faithful and True, and in righteousness <u>he doth judge and make war</u>. His eyes were as a flame of fire, and on his head were many crowns; and he had a name written, that no man knew, but he himself. And he was clothed with a vesture *dipped in blood: and his name is called The Word of God."*

At the very end of the seven year Tribulation, Christ returns to Earth as the Lion of the Tribe of Judah, destroys the armies of the Antichrist and sets up His throne in Jerusalem to rule the world. As you would expect, you see it happening right there around the end of the book...

...and also right here in chapter fourteen:

Revelation 14:19-20, "And the angel thrust in his sickle into the earth, and gathered the vine of the earth, and cast it into the great winepress of the wrath of God. And the winepress was trodden without the city, and <u>blood came out of the winepress, even unto the horse bridles</u>, by the space of a thousand and six hundred furlongs."

While it's not quite as clear here as it was in chapter nineteen, blood coming up to the horse bridles can be nothing else than Armageddon. The "vine of the earth" is the Antichrist. That's Armageddon twice so far, but it doesn't stop there.

Revelation 11:15-18 "And the seventh angel sounded; and there were great voices in heaven, saying, <u>The kingdoms of this world are become the kingdoms of our Lord,</u> and of his Christ; and he shall reign for ever and ever. And the four and twenty elders, which sat before God on their seats, fell upon their faces, and worshipped God, Saying, We give thee thanks, O Lord God Almighty, which art, and wast, and art to come; because <u>thou hast taken to thee thy great power,</u> and hast reigned.

7

And the nations were angry, and thy wrath is come, and <u>the time of the dead, that they should be judged</u>, and that thou shouldest give reward unto thy servants the prophets, and to the saints, and them that fear thy name, small and great; and shouldest destroy them which destroy the earth."

Did you see the part about the kingdoms of this world becoming the kingdoms of Christ, and the dead being judged? The dead are judged in Revelation 20:12 as well. Does this mean they are judged twice? Of course they're not. We're seeing the same events happening for the third time.

Now if you're still not quite convinced...

Revelation 6:14-17, "And the <u>heaven departed as a scroll when it is rolled together</u>; and every mountain and island were moved out of their places. And the kings of the earth, and the great men, and the rich men, and the chief captains, and the mighty men, and every bondman, and every free man, hid themselves in the dens and in the rocks of the mountains; And said to the mountains and rocks, Fall on us, and <u>hide us from the face of him</u> that sitteth on the throne, and from the wrath of the Lamb: For <u>the great day of his wrath is come</u>; and who shall be able to stand?"

So, the great day of His wrath is come at the beginning of the book, in chapter six? At the beginning of the book you have captains and mighty men hiding and running from the face of Jesus Christ? All of these things are supposed to happen at the end of the story, but we see it here in chapter six!

Looking at the map at the beginning of this chapter you'll see a basic idea how Revelation is divided up. The first road is the Rapture Road, and it changes names to Seal Street and continues through the Tribulation up to the Second Advent (or Armageddon). *During the Seals Jesus is the Lamb who was slain, opens the book, and brings His wrath to Earth.*

The second road is called Witness Way; it begins in the middle of the Tribulation and ends at Armageddon. *During the Trumpets, Jesus is the Mighty Angel who roars as a lion, completes the mystery of God, and anoints His two witnesses.*

Route 666 also comes off Seal Street at the middle of the Tribulation and it ends at Armageddon as well. *During the personages, Jesus is the Man-Child who is born, ascends unto Heaven, and returns to rule with a rod of iron.*

The last road, the King's Highway, starts well past the middle of the Tribulation but still before the advent, and goes clear on out to the Everlasting Kingdom. *During the Vials, He is the Word of God who destroys Babylon, in righteousness judges and makes war, and creates all things new.*

The Antichrist is portrayed in four ways throughout Revelation as well. During the Seals he is the man on the White Horse who imitates Christ. During the Trumpets he is the Beast that ascends out of the Bottomless Pit and makes war with the two witnesses. During the personages, he is the Beast of the Sea who the world worships. Lastly, during the Vials he is the Beast that makes war with the Lamb.

Now that we understand the pitfalls of studying Revelation the wrong way, and now that we see the four roads on the Revelation roadmap, let's get started on the first one, the road to the Rapture.

CHAPTER TWO

THE ROAD TO RAPTURE

"He that hath an ear, let him hear
what the Spirit saith unto the
churches."
Revelation 3:13

PART ONE OF THE FIRST ACCOUNT
Revelation 1:1-3:22

THE CHURCH AGE

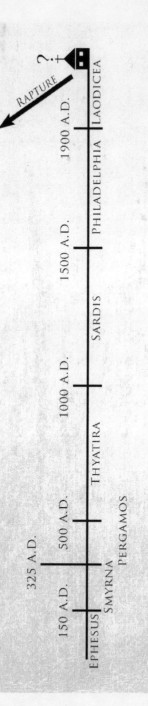

EPHESUS
SMYRNA
PERGAMOS
THYATIRA
SARDIS
PHILADELPHIA
LAODICEA

150 A.D.
325 A.D.
500 A.D.
1000 A.D.
1500 A.D.
1900 A.D.

RAPTURE

I. Understanding the Vision

Revelation starts with John receiving a vision on the isle of Patmos. He sees the vision from beginning to end as it is written, with most things being actual literal events that will take place in the future, and some things being symbols of other personages, peoples, things, etc, that will also appear in the future. It's important to understand the differences.

Here's an example of something symbolic:

Revelation 17:18, "And <u>the woman</u> which thou sawest is that great city, which reineth over the kings of the earth."

If the text says John saw a woman then that's exactly what he saw. That doesn't mean that is what it meant though, it represented something else. Now, if you read chapter one you know you have to be careful about taking things symbolically; it's always best to take the passage as literally as possible. However, based upon actual wording in other passages you can clearly see that the whore in Revelation is a *city* (see Revelation 17:18).

Another example of this is the sea that the Beast comes out of in Rev. 13:1. In ***Rev. 17:15*** the same sea can be taken as "...***peoples, and multitudes, and nations, and tongues***" because that is what the verse interprets the sea as being. It's best to allow Scripture to interpret Scripture.

Take care when interpreting things symbolically. There are those that try to make the man on the horse in chapter six *(the Antichrist)* the Man on the horse in chapter nineteen *(Jesus Christ)*, or the woman in chapter twelve *(Israel)* to be Mary or the church. Obviously we should not just believe what someone tells us without checking it out for ourselves, and we shouldn't base rock-hard doctrine on something that isn't clear.

II. The Futurist Interpretation of the Churches

There are a few ways to look at the seven churches. **The first and most obvious way is to read it exactly how it's written**: a letter to seven different churches that were all unique at the time.

The second way is to spiritually apply it to you. What kind of Christian are you? Are you an Ephesian Christian? Zealous, but lost your first love? Are you lukewarm in your Christianity, compromising with the world in doctrine and standards, are you Laodicean? We should all strive to be Philadelphian Christians, holding fast to the word of God while loving the brethren at the same time.

The third way of interpretation is to also look at the churches prophetically. This is a very common teaching and accepted by many futurists. It is that the seven churches are in fact seven rough periods of time throughout the last 2,000 years of church history. Here is what the seven names of these churches actually mean:

Ephesus: "Fully Purposed"
Smyrna: "Myrrh"

Pergamos: "Much Marriage"
Thyatira: "Odor of Affliction"
Sardis: "Red Ones"
Philadelphia: "Brotherly Love"
Laodicea: "The Rights of the People"

Here are some of the similarities between church history and these seven churches:

1. The Ephesian church in Revelation lost its first love. The early church, though zealous, was also infiltrated by Greek philosophy which took the heart out of much of the church and replaced it with ecclesiastical and non-biblical traditions.

2. The Smyrna church was the persecuted church that was faithful unto death in Revelation. It was told that it would have particular tribulation for ten days. The corresponding time period would be what follows the early church, which was a time of great suffering under Pagan Rome. The most devastating of the persecution was ten years under Diocletian and ten specific persecutions under Pagan Rome.

3. The Pergamos church was accused of compromising with the world in Revelation. Following the persecution the church became accepted by the world and Christianity became the state religion. Hence Pergamos means "much marriage," as the church became married to the world and began growing cold, heretical and elitist. We see the rise of the Roman Catholic Church. This corresponds to the Pergamos church having its troubles with the doctrine

15

of Balaam and the Nicolaitans, an unbiblical clergy-laity system.

4. **The Thyatira church** had a huge problem with a woman named Jezebel who was teaching false doctrine, fornicating and worshipping idols. This is the primary subject for the message to the Thyatira church. This corresponds to the darkest time in the history of the church when the Roman Catholic Church ruled the world with an iron fist. She taught false doctrine, controlled governments with spiritual fornication and taught idol worship. Anyone who opposed her was murdered, ergo Thyatira means "odor of affliction."

5. **The Sardis church** was backslidden and dead in the eyes of God, but He also said that there were *"...a few names even in Sardis which have not defiled their garments..."* This ties in with the middle of the Dark Ages up through the Great Reformation. It was during this period of time that a few "red ones" (Sardis means "red ones") stood up and led movements against the Roman Catholic Church. The "red ones" shed their blood so we could have a Bible today in our own language.

6. **The Philadelphia church** was the only church that received nothing but commendations from Jesus. They had an open door and nothing stood in their way to fully going after the Great Commission. This ties into the greatest missionary period of church history ever, which followed the Great Reformation. The church was afire for Christ, Christians lived holy lives

and loved each other, and God brought revivals all over the world.

7. **The Laodicean church** was the only church about which God had nothing good to say. It was more concerned with material possessions than souls. Its definition was "the rights of the people." It thought of itself as something when Christ said it was wretched, miserable, poor, blind and naked. This is the time period we are in now, a period of full apostasy. Christians spend more on dog food than they do missions. While they'll let their TV say anything it wants to, their preachers are taught from early on to not rock the boat and to bring friendly messages of relationships and pop psychology instead of authoritative Bible preaching from the word of God.

It should be abundantly clear at this point that these seven churches are not just seven churches that John wrote to; they picture seven loose periods of time over the last 2,000 years. Some of the these periods naturally overlap each other as you would expect from gradual changes throughout history, and some have clear-cut turning points. As we lead up to the Rapture, let's take a closer look at these time periods and the heroes of them.

III. Imperial Persecution of the Church

The first church John wrote to was the church at **Ephesus**. This time period goes from the time of Christ to about 150 A.D.

The Apostolic Age shows us some amazing Christians, as every age has: from the apostle Peter who asked to be crucified upside down because he felt himself unworthy to be crucified like Christ, to the martyr Ignatius who shook his fist and dared hungry lions in the coliseum to grind his bones to powder. These men were the first to suffer for Christ.

There was Polycarp, who, though tied to the stake, wouldn't catch fire until he had been killed with a sword. And one could never forget the apostle Paul with his 195 whip drawn scars, and whose *"...bodily presence is weak, and his speech contemptible..."* (II Cor. 10:10), claimed like no other man, *"I bear in my body the marks of the Lord Jesus."*

They labored and never fainted. However, as is so easily the case, many in that time period began to lose what God called their first love as the philosophies of carnal men crept into the church.

Following the period of Ephesus, **the Smyrna Period** (150-325 A.D.) was also a period of great persecution. The Roman Empire had turned its sword towards Christianity in an effort to wipe it out.

As if trying to escape the pagan Roman government wasn't enough trouble, there were huge problems within what was then thought of as "Christendom" with false apostles, the Nicolaitans.

During these times some groups of Christians known as the Novatians *and Montanists* arose to challenge the Nicolaitans. The Nicolaitans taught the total supremacy of what was an immoral clergy, and that mankind would eventually bring in peace on

Earth. However the Novatians and Montanists believed Christ was coming back one day to set up His kingdom on Earth without the aid of man; they also refused to practice infant baptism, and they only baptized adult believers.

Christians suffered tremendously under the imperial fist of Rome. It was their desire to be holy and separated that got them killed. Back then, anyone naming the name of Christ was killed for it! Even men that Bible believers today would define as heretics made other people so *uncomfortable* and *convicted* (modern day Christianity has lost what even the heretics had back then, the biblical doctrine of separation) about their wicked lifestyles, that they were martyred. One such example is the man Cyprian. He taught several Catholic fundamentals and was martyred just for being religious. Unfortunately, his martyrdom later led to people taking the heresies that Cyprian taught and exalting them to a status above the word of God.

Revelation 2:10, "Fear none of those things which thou shalt suffer: behold, the devil shall cast some of you into prison, that ye may be tried; and <u>*ye shall have tribulation ten days*</u>*: be thou faithful unto death, and I will give thee a crown of life."*

The Smyrna church was prophesied to go through ten days of persecution. This corresponds to the ten official persecutions by the pagan Roman government:

1) Nero (64 A.D.)
2) Domitian (90-96 A.D.)
3) Trajan (98-117 A.D.)

4) Hadrian (117-138 A.D.)
5) Marcus Aurelius (161-181 A.D.)
6) Septimus Severus (202-211 A.D.)
7) Maximus the Thracian (235-251 A.D.)
8) Decius (249-251 A.D.)
9) Valerian (257-260 A.D.)
10) Diocletian / Galerius (303-311 A.D.)

Not only were there ten actual periods of suffering for Christians under pagan Rome, but there were ten years of unique and extreme suffering under Diocletian. Following this, a new era was brought in by a man named Constantine.

IV. The World Falls into Darkness

This time was known as **the Pergamos Church Period**, and it spanned from 325 to 500 A.D.

Constantine invaded and took over Rome. With a vision of a cross using the Greek letters Rho and Chi, and the promise to *"in this sign conquer,"* he won the Battle of Milvian Bridge in 313 A.D.

Upon his "conversion" to Christendom, he immediately stopped the persecution of Christians throughout the empire. Naturally, the church rejoiced.

Then in 325 A.D., something really sinister happened. Constantine decided to make what he believed to be Christianity the religion of Rome in what was called the council of Nicea. This is when the Roman Catholic Church really started.

Pergamos means "much marriage," and it was during this time period that the church was married to the world. Persecution died down, and so did soul winning as Christians spent much of their time arguing instead of working. Augustine, a famed church father of this period, wrote a book called *"The City of God."* In it he tried to tell us that Rome was the city of God, and that the one thousand year millennial reign of Christ had begun now that Constantine had stopped all persecution.

Still there were, as there always have been, some fireballs for the Lord in those days - the most ironic being Patrick of Ireland, who preached to natives that salvation was by grace through faith alone in the shed blood of Jesus Christ. *He was anything but a Catholic.* The Catholic Church did exactly what the Pharisees did in Matt. 23:29-33: they pretended that Patrick was one of theirs and made him a saint!

Becoming more powerful, the whore of Revelation 17 and 18 begins putting out the light of the gospel any way she can. This is the period known as Thyatira, and it covers 500-1000 A.D. Real preachers were few and far between as the world fell into darkness.

During this time the idea of post-Millennialism was introduced. This is basically the idea that mankind will bring in the thousand years of peace. It is an unbiblical teaching that saps the evangelistic fervor out of people. That fervor is present in people when they believe Jesus could come back *today*.

During this period is when the Dark Ages began; the Catholic Church held its grip on the world so

21

tightly that very few dared to stand against it. Free thought was stifled, as was the word of God. People started worshipping Mary, and Popes issued curses and blessings in whatever way helped them the most politically.

Then came in **the Sardis Church Period** (1000-1500 A.D.), and during it the Great Reformation. Christ said of this church in *Rev 3:1, "...thou hast a name that thou livest, and art dead."* That's because many of the true believers were still Catholic as far as church membership, and though they were part a powerful church they were part of a dead church.

In this period of time, the Roman Church was at its greatest peak of power. It did not hesitate to burn Christians at the stake for things like re-baptizing a new believer, believing the wafer was only symbolic and not the literal body of Jesus Christ, speaking out against corrupt Catholic Church practices, refusing to worship Mary, or refusing to sprinkle babies. In one such instance, the Roman Church gave out medals to Catholics for murdering Protestants during what was called the "St. Bartholomew Day Massacre." The demon-possessed Popes didn't care who they killed, be it woman or child. All over the world, they murdered millions of Christians in the name of Christ.

According to Foxe's Book of Martyrs, they killed and tortured in the most depraved and sickest ways possible. Some items on the list of atrocities the Catholic organization is guilty include the burning of people at the stake, removing fingernails with burning hot tongs, the cutting off of body parts and then searing the stumps to stop blood loss as well as many other things. We need to be reminded from time to time of the price that others have paid.

V. The Chains are Broken

John Wycliffe, *"the morning star of the Reformation,"* was born in 1320. He taught the idea that if something wasn't in the Bible that it was false. Mr. Wycliffe felt strongly enough about that idea to translate the Bible from Latin into the common language of the day: English. Instead of the Bible being some dark and hidden mystical document, now everyone could have it, read it, and see the truth for themselves. This is what really got the ball rolling, because when people started reading the Bible for themselves they began taking stands against the Catholic Church.

As fast as the Roman Church could kill them, they kept popping up under names such as *"Anabaptists," "Waldendsians," "Cathari," "Albigenses,"* and others. They loved the word of God and they were willing to die for what they believed. From John Wycliffe in 1370 to John Huss in 1415, down to the Italian *Girolamo Savonarola* in 1498, and eventually to the man that in the early part of the 1500s broke the back of the Church of Rome, *Martin Luther.*

Luther attacked the doctrines of the Catholic Church with such fervor that he could not be ignored by the world:

"If there were nothing else to show that the Pope is Antichrist, this would be enough. Dost thou hear this, O Pope! not [sic] the most holy, but the most sinful? Would that God would hurl thy chair headlong from heaven, and cast it down into the abyss of hell! Who gave you the power to exalt yourself above your God; to break and to loose what He has commanded; to teach Christians, more especially Germans who are of noble nature, and are famed in all histories for uprightness and truth, to be false, unfaithful, perjured, treacherous, and wicked? ...and through your mouth and your pen Satan lies as he never lied before, teaching you to twist and pervert the Scriptures according to your own arbitrary will. O Lord Christ, look down upon this; let Thy [sic] day of judgment come and destroy the devil's lair at Rome." (Address to the Nobility of the German Nation Respecting the Reformation of the Christian Estate by Martin Luther)

Addressing the Pope as "your hellishness" and "most hellish father," he broke down the door of religious slavery. He did this by using the power of the printed page with the Ninety-Five Thesis, pamphlets, and a translation of the Bible into German. He became so powerful that the Roman Church couldn't stop him and later on in life he died peacefully in the presence of his friends and family.

Now with power of the Roman Church broken, in came the **Philadelphia Church Period**! This time period stretched for 400 years, from 1500 to around 1900 A.D. The peoples of the world had Bibles, and they had missionaries to preach them the word. There were men like William Carey, Jonathan Goforth, Adoniram Judson, and Hudson Taylor.

These men went into the difficult areas of the world to bring the gospel, and the spiritual oppression that the Catholic Church had held over the world was gone. Christ said this church had an open door and that they kept His word. Now with the word of God being so widespread, the minds and hearts of men were enlightened and prepared for the gospel like never before.

More people were saved in this time period than any other, with the Authorized King James version of the Bible coming into existence in 1611.

There was *John Wesley* who kept the nation of England from a bloody revolution and *George Whitefield* who preached to thousands on the plains and in the streets of America. In the English speaking world there was unity around the King James Bible; those that were setting the world on fire for Christ believed it, saw its fruit, and never questioned its accuracy and authority.

VI. A New Front

The only thing the Devil could do at this point was to start attacking the book that did it all. Only instead of killing the proponents of it and hiding it, he decided to counterfeit it. In came **Laodicea** (1900 to today). The church thought they were rich, but they were poor, needy, wretched, blind and miserable. Man started getting too big for his britches with ideas like

25

Darwinism. The critical point was when *Wescott* and *Hort* introduced Catholic manuscripts to be translated for the new Bible they were writing.

Instead of choosing to base their Revised Version off of the Antiochian manuscripts that were soaked in the blood of martyrs and filled with the Holy Spirit, they choose the dusty, vain, and corrupt Siniaticus and Vaticanus of Egypt and Rome. Other than a few, such as the NKJV (which uses both sets of manuscripts), most new English versions since then have followed the same example. They remove and alter key doctrinal verses that Christians need to understand to defend their faith.

This era is not without its preachers though! Billy Sunday left a baseball career to preach against sin, closing down bars in the towns he preached at with thousands trusting Christ. There was *J. Frank Norris* who raised millions of dollars for Christ during the Great Depression and saw tens of thousands saved.

There was *Lester Roloff* who refused to take a license from the government and put to shame government-run facilities that pretended to reform the lives of troubled youths. His homes were run according to biblical principles and the kids came out new creatures in Christ. He preached, sang, started churches and schools, and died serving Christ.

To mention the men and women that carried the word of God throughout the Church Age would take many books; we haven't even scratched the surface.

Towards the end of this era the enfeebling influence of these watered-down corrupt versions began to be felt. Also with advancements in technology, information was streamed at rapid rates through telephone, radio, television, and eventually the Internet. With this advancement in technology, the sinful nature of man was spread at a more efficient rate as well.

At the close of the Laodicean Age, Bible believers fought through the darkness for revival as much as they could. Many of them believed that worldwide revival was impossible at this point, and some took the attitude that even on a local basis it wasn't going to happen. Whether they believed revival was possible or not, they still fought on the best they could in their cities, towns, villages and countries.

Then one day it happened. A missionary preaching in a village in Africa, a young couple out on visitation in America on a Saturday afternoon, some Christian in a far-off country facing torture for not renouncing the name of Christ – they and the rest of the world were all suddenly interrupted, in whatever it was they were doing at that particular moment. The heavens split open, a light was seen across the entire world all at the same instant of time, a trumpet sounded...

...and they were gone.

I Corinthians 15:51-58, "Behold, I shew you a mystery; We shall not all sleep, but we shall all be changed, In a moment, in the twinkling of an eye, at the last trump: for the trumpet shall sound, and the dead shall be raised incorruptible, and we shall be changed. For this corruptible must put on incorruption, and this mortal must put on

27

immortality. So when this corruptible shall have put on incorruption, and this mortal shall have put on immortality, then shall be brought to pass the saying that is written, Death is swallowed up in victory. O death, where is thy sting? O grave, where is thy victory? The sting of death is sin; and the strength of sin is the law. But thanks be to God, which giveth us the victory through our Lord Jesus Christ. Therefore, my beloved brethren, be ye stedfast, unmoveable, always abounding in the work of the Lord, forasmuch as ye know that your labour is not in vain in the Lord."

CHAPTER THREE

SEAL STREET

"And when ye shall see Jerusalem compassed with armies, then know that the desolation thereof is nigh."
Luke 21:20

PART TWO OF THE FIRST ACCOUNT
Revelation 4:1-8:1

THE SEVEN SEALS

"THE BEGINNING OF SORROWS"   "THE GREAT TRIBULATION"

1ST YEAR	2ND YEAR	3RD YEAR	4TH YEAR	5TH YEAR	6TH YEAR

SECOND ADVENT →

← RAPTURE OF THE CHURCH

✡ 1ST SEAL- WHITE HORSE/COVENANT SIGNED/RISE OF ANTICHRIST

✡ 2ND SEAL- RED HORSE/WAR

✡ 3RD SEAL- BLACK HORSE/FAMINE

RUSSIA ATTACKS ISRAEL

✡ 4TH SEAL- PALE HORSE/COVENANT BROKEN

✡ 5TH SEAL- MARTYRS

✡ 6TH SEAL- PRE-ARMAGEDDON

✡ 7TH SEAL- SECOND ADVENT/SILENCE IN HEAVEN

✡ = BEGINNING OF SEAL

I. John's Pre-Tribulation Rapture

Chapter four begins with John being caught up straight into Heaven before the Tribulation begins. This is a picture of how it will be for the church. Many teach a church rapture in the middle of the Tribulation, or even the end of the Tribulation, but the truth is we'll be raptured out of here before *Jacob's Trouble* begins. In the first three chapters of Revelation *John is on Earth*, and then right before the Tribulation begins he is caught up into Heaven. After being mentioned in Revelation 1-3, the church (or the Bride) isn't mentioned again until after the Tribulation in Rev.18, and in Rev. 19 she's already in Heaven with Jesus before the Second Advent.

Besides being taken up into Heaven before the Tribulation, John is a picture of the church because:

1. John is called "John the beloved," and he constantly refers to himself as the disciple whom Jesus loved. The church is beloved of Christ.

2. John's gospel emphasizes faith in Jesus as the Son of God more than any other, as the Church Age emphasizes faith more than any other age.

3. John is the only apostle that was not martyred; the church is saved from the wrath to come.

4. John is the only apostle that was promised to witness the Second Coming in his lifetime; the church is given the promise of the Blessed Hope.

ROADMAP THROUGH REVELATION

There's no such thing as a mid-Tribulation or post-Tribulation Rapture of what we know to be the church.*

The Bible says in I *Thessalonians 1:10, "And to wait for his Son from heaven, whom he raised from the dead, even Jesus, <u>which delivered us from the wrath to come</u>."* In this verse Paul is writing about a future wrath tied to the Tribulation, which is abundantly clear by the context of the passage.

[*The post-Tribulation Rapture passage is Matt. 24:30-31. In that passage Christ is physically visible in the sky, and then a rapture follows. In Rev. 19 the Bride is with Christ before Heaven is opened, and then as Jesus comes down to Earth He is visible in the sky. The church is already in Heaven and comes down with Jesus Christ before this rapture in Matthew 24 happens. These are two separate raptures for two different groups of people.

Contrary to what post and mid-Tribulation theorists would have you to believe, the pre-Tribulation teaching did not originate with Darby and Scofield in the 1800s. Ephraem the Syrian was a respected and well known Christian writer of his day. In the book, *On the Last Times, the Antichrist, and the End of the World*, written 373 A.D., he states, *"For all the saints and Elect of God are gathered, prior to the tribulation that is to come, and are taken to the Lord lest they see the confusion that is to overwhelm the world because of our sins."*]

Many claim that this just means that we are raptured before the wrath of God is poured out on the

Earth, supposing that the second half of the Tribulation or the last one third of it is when God's wrath finally hits. The problem with that thinking is that there is plenty of wrath in the first part of the Tribulation! You have the Red Horse stomping around the world *"...to take peace from the earth..."* and follow that right up with the Black Horse and worldwide famine. This is the wrath of God that is to come from which we are delivered. Nowhere in the Bible does it say that there are three and a half straight years of peace; it only says that the Antichrist uses the message of peace to get what he wants. "The beginning of sorrows" in Mt. 24:4-8 is the lighter side of the Tribulation, but in it you still have famine, disease, and war.

Christ said in **Rev. 3:10, "Because thou hast kept the word of my patience, I also will keep thee from the hour of temptation, which shall come upon all the world, to try them that dwell upon the earth."**

This shows that Christ's church will not experience the *"...hour of temptation which shall come upon all the world..."* What else could that time be but the Tribulation? What other time, from the time of John's writing till now, has *the entire world* been tried but the Christians saved from it? It is very clear that the trial we are saved from here is the Tribulation.

I John 14 Jesus spoke of believers as having *"a place prepared"* for them, and then we see in Isaiah 26:20 the Lord say, **"Come, my people, enter thou into thy chambers, and shut thy doors about thee: hide thyself as it were for a little moment, until the** *indignation be overpast."* This passage has double-application to the Tribulation Jews hiding in Petra (we'll see that later) but also to the Christians who are in their chambers, that is, in *the place prepared for them* in Heaven during the Tribulation.

There is a lot of debate out there about the timing Rapture of the church and there always will be. The reason that traditionally people believe in a pre-Tribulation view is because there is simply more ammunition on that side of the battlefield. We've already looked at a few passages, but consider I Thess. 5:9 which tells us that *"God hath not appointed us to wrath..."* or Romans 5:9 that reminds us that we're saved from wrath. Consider the elders in Revelation 4 that clearly picture the church – up in Heaven before the Tribulation.

Jeremiah 30:7 and Daniel 9 identify the Tribulation as being **a)** the seventieth week and **b)** the time of Jacob's trouble. What does that mean? It means that it is Jewish in nature; it has nothing to do with the church! God is picking up right where He left off with and bringing Israel to a place of repentance. They *will* accept Jesus as their Messiah this time. To further solidify this, when one compares the last days of the church (II Tim.3) you find *apostasy*, but when you look at Israel's last days (Joel 2:27-32) they end in *revival*. Israel's last days are revival because they've turned to Christ; the church's last days are apostasy because they've turned to the world. They cannot both be the same group of people, they cannot both be in the Tribulation, and they cannot both be under the same

34

program. The church is pulled out of the world before the seven-year Tribulation begins!

Nowhere in the Bible does it specifically say that the Tribulation begins immediately after the Rapture happens, but it does begin the moment the ink is dry on a peace treaty orchestrated by the Antichrist *for Israel.* Why is that? It's because the Tribulation is all about the nation of Israel and their relationship to their Messiah. This is abundantly clear when one reads the book of Daniel. The book of Daniel is the companion book to Revelation. You can't study Revelation without taking a look at Daniel, and you can't study Daniel without Revelation. The Jews rejected Christ the first time He came, but they will accept Him the second time because their hearts will be turned back to God.

What would the church be doing in a situation like that? We didn't reject Christ; Israel did. So why would we be going through any part of a time period strictly designated as the time period that God chastens Israel and brings her back to Him? The promises made to Abraham (Genesis 15 and 22) have to do with the *nation of Israel* and they *must* be fulfilled, and for those promises to be fulfilled Israel must repent.

We are told to look for Christ to come back soon (Titus 2:13). We are not told to look for anything else but Christ coming back soon.

If we're to go through the miserable first three and a half years of the Tribulation, then wouldn't it be expected that we should be looking for the Antichrist to appear, and all the other things that should appear

35

with him? Shouldn't we be busy stuffing beef jerky into our mattresses and building a bunker in the backyard? No, our hope is in Jesus Christ coming back soon and our job is to stay busy in the meantime doing everything we can for Him - and not to worry about the Tribulation.

II. Babies and the Rapture

Along those same lines, people often wonder about children when it comes to the Rapture. Will the little ones go up or will they stay? The doctrine of the age of accountability teaches that a child that is not able to trust Christ because he simply doesn't understand sin and righteousness is not held accountable in the eyes of God. In other words, when a baby dies *its soul is clean and its spirit is alive* – it goes to Heaven. David knew he would see his son again in II Sam. 12:23.

Rom. 7:9, *"For **I was alive without the law once**: but when the commandment came, sin revived, and I died."*

Paul said he was alive before the commandment came. He was talking about his spirit being alive, just like Adam and Eve before the fall. The commandment coming is when Paul reached the point in his heart that he knew he was guilty before God. In good churches all over America there are little boys and girls who want to "ask Jesus" because they love Him and have heard so much about Him, but they have no concept of sin and righteousness and *therefore they can't,* even though they would if they could.

Rom. 5:13, "(For until the law sin was in the world: but sin is not imputed when there is no law." This verse is another example of how sin is not imputed to a person when they have no knowledge of the law. God puts a law within our hearts: our conscience. While little ones oftentimes do understand that some actions are bad and will result in parental discipline, the knowledge of sin before a holy God doesn't exist yet.

According to Jesus Christ in Matthew 24:21 the Tribulation is by far the worst, most dreadful and cataclysmic period of time, with nothing even coming close to it before or after. It is God's judgment on a wicked human race that has rejected Him. There's no way that He's going to let a child, who couldn't trust Jesus if he or she wanted to, go into the Tribulation.

When there is a way out for little ones to avoid judgment meant for the parents, God uses it. In Numbers, the little ones were allowed to go into the Promised Land even though the parents were not.

Num. 14:31-32, "But your little ones, which ye said should be a prey, them will I bring in, and they shall know the land which ye have despised. But as for you, your carcases, they shall fall in this wilderness."

This is demonstrable evidence of how God handles little ones during judgment when there is a way out for them. They are "safe," they are not punished for the actions of their parents, and they are not *punished* for not being *able* to accept Jesus.

37

After all this, consider lastly an emotional yet valid argument. If our children were to remain on the Earth to suffer needlessly and die terrible deaths, or worse yet to accept the mark and go to Hell, it would no doubt defy the very nature of the promise that the Rapture is our "Blessed Hope." God put within us an amazing love for our children, and He loves them even more than we do.

III. John in Heaven

John stands in utter amazement of Heaven, as we all will. He sees the throne, the four beasts, the sea of glass, and seven candles burning before the throne. When you read this chapter, try to put yourself in the place that John was. One moment, he was a slave on the Isle of Patmos, the next he is in Heaven before the throne of God.

In the last verse of chapter four we see the answer to the age old question: **Why am I here?** Well, here is the answer...

Revelation 4:11, "Thou art worthy, O Lord, to receive glory and honour and power: for thou hast created all things, and for <u>thy pleasure they are and were created</u>."

We were all created for the sole purpose of bringing pleasure to God. Our thoughts, actions, motives – all of life should be lived in light of that fact! The reason many people don't feel complete or fulfilled is because they're not following Revelation 4:11.

In chapter five, the Lamb is the only one worthy to open the book and loose the Seals. Everyone praises Him for opening the Seals. In Heaven, praising Him is all we'll want to do for a very long time. After all the hurt we've caused Him, won't it be great to finally be able to praise him throughout all eternity without the hampering of sin on us?

IV. The Judgment Seat of Christ

Before we go further in the timeline, we need to look at the event that will be taking place up in Heaven during the first half of the Tribulation. In the middle of the Tribulation there will be a wonderful wedding, complete with guests, a Bride, a Bridegroom, and even a best man. Before that happens, the Bride of Christ, the church, has to go through a judgment called the Judgment Seat of Christ.

This Judgment can be found in *II Cor. 5:10, "For we must all appear before the judgment seat of Christ; that every one may receive the things done in his body, according to that he hath done, whether it be good or bad."*

The main text for this judgment is I Cor. 3. In that chapter you'll see that the Christian is judged based upon his works that were done while he was in his earthly body. This has absolutely nothing to do with salvation and whether or not the Christian goes to Heaven or Hell. He is not judged according to his sins; it is his works that are judged. They are either good or bad.

The rewards given to the Christian are gold, silver, and precious stones. There are several ideas about what sort of works earn what kind of rewards. As good a teaching as any is that gold (deity) represents praise to God, silver (price of redemption) represents witnessing, and precious stones are for actual souls won to Christ. The wood, hay, and stubble are for works done in the flesh.

The Christian can also earn five crowns:

1. The Crown of Righteousness is for loving the appearing of the Lord Jesus Christ. It is for looking forward to and loving the Rapture. It means not hoping you get married first, or you retire first, or you get right first – it means when you get up in the morning your hope and prayer is that Jesus Christ will come back *that day*. II Tim. 4:8

2. The Crown of Life is for resisting temptation and dying as a martyr. It is commonly called the "Martyr's Crown." James 1:12, Rev. 2:10

3. The Crown of Rejoicing is for soul winning, also called the "Soul Winner's Crown." Could you imagine living your whole life as a Christian without leading one person to the Lord? I Thess. 2:19

4. The Incorruptible Crown is for living a life of temperance, controlling your flesh, and resisting temptation. I Cor. 9:24-27

5. The Crown of Glory is for honest and faithful pastors who are not hirelings. If you are so blessed as to have one of these as your pastor, you should treat him with love, respect and grace. Many Christians have "grace" (if that's what you want to call it) with their TV and the books they read, all the while ingesting a boatload full of profanity, nudity, and adult situations – and then those same Christians seem to turn on their preachers so easily.

A preacher, whether he is a pastor, evangelist, or missionary, is called to regularly put himself out there and risk ridicule for the cause of Christ. He's an imperfect man called to do an impossible task: represent the Lord Jesus Christ and the word of God with passion. I Peter 5:1-4

Before you trust Christ the only thing that matters is getting saved. After you are saved, the only thing that matters is the Judgment Seat of Christ. Whether we agree with the idea or not, we will be held accountable for how we lived our saved lives and we will be juded.

Do you want to stand before the Holy Trinity and be told that you did a lousy job? You will be judged on how you used your time, talents and treasure for the cause of Christ. Do you want every Christian that ever lived to see you judged as having wasted your life on self? It is a terrifying thought, and it should be.

II Cor. 5:10-11, "For we must all appear before the judgment seat of Christ; that every one may receive the things done in his body, according to that he hath done, whether it be good or bad. <u>Knowing therefore the terror of the Lord</u>, we persuade men; but we are made manifest unto God;

and I trust also are made manifest in your consciences."

On the other hand, nothing could be better than to kneel before the Lord Jesus Christ as He lays a crown on your head and proclaims, *"Well done, my good and faithful servant."* That would beat any award you've ever earned in this life, it makes the championships of the greatest sports look like nothing. Forget a gold Olympic medal, the Stanley Cup or the Vince Lombari Trophy!

People spend their lives amassing power, fame and riches. Christians do the same. As a Christian, every decision you make in life needs to be in light of the Judgment Seat of Christ. Your education won't mean a thing at this judgment, and your bank account won't either. If that is what you live for, you are wasting your life. If making more money means moving your family away from a good church, and in the meantime you lose your kids to the world, you just earned yourself nothing at this judgment. If compromising on standards for convenience ruins your family and kids, you've earned nothing. If you get your feelings hurt and leave church, and your whole family goes down the tubes, you just ruined your chances at this judgment.

The only thing that matters for a Christian *is* the Judgment Seat of Christ. Are you living your life in light of the judgment?

CHAPTER THREE: SEAL STREET

V. The First Three Seals

Have you ever been driving down a road, and then it all of a sudden changed names? We are still on the first account, but the name of the road has been changed from Rapture Road to Seal Street because we're past the Rapture now. The first road begins with the first church period (Ephesus) right after Christ's crucifixion, and it continues on down through a couple thousand years of history, past where we are today, and into the future with the Rapture of the church. Then it goes through all seven of the Seals, ending with the Seventh Seal. The Seals can help to understand the entire Tribulation in a nutshell because it basically is an overview of the whole seven years.

The First Seal brings in a White Horse with a rider that carries a bow and conquers. The odd thing is that he manages to do it without any arrows. This rider is the Antichrist (not everyone riding a white horse is a good guy). The reason he lacks arrows is because he assumes his power by trickery, manipulation and great speeches of peace.

Part of the way the Antichrist suddenly ascends to power in the beginning of the Tribulation is by becoming the leader of ten federated nations. This is the old Roman Empire revived (the feet and legs of the image in Daniel 2 were Rome, with the iron and clay feet being the Antichrist's kingdom). In Revelation 13 it speaks of the Beast (the Antichrist) having ten horns and Daniel interprets the horns to be kings. The Antichrist reaches the height of his power towards the

43

middle of the Tribulation, but obviously he is very powerful thrughout the entire period.

In Revelation 17:7 it is clear that there is a close relationship between the Beast (the first horseman) and the Catholic Church - they use each other as he goes forth conquering and to conquer.

In Daniel the Antichrist is called the "King of Fierce Countenance." The Pope is a king – he sits on a throne, wears a crown, and rules over a literal country (Vatican City) in Europe as well as over the consciences of millions across the globe. The Vatican always has and always will work to control as much of the world as it can.

Daniel 9 contains the strongest indicator of the Antichrist's national origin, and it's not Iran or America:

Daniel 9:26-27, "And after threescore and two weeks shall Messiah be cut off, but not for himself: and the people of the prince that shall come shall destroy the city and the sanctuary; and the end thereof shall be with a flood, and unto the end of the war desolations are determined.

27) And he shall confirm the covenant with many for one week: and in the midst of the week he shall cause the sacrifice and the oblation to cease, and for the overspreading of abominations he shall make it desolate, even until the consummation, and that determined shall be poured upon the desolate."

In verse 27 we see the Antichrist making a covenant with the people of the world, and with Israel.

This covenant lasts for one week of years, that is seven years. Now after understanding that take a look at the name that is given for the Antichrist in verse 26: He is called *"the prince that shall come."* What does all this have to do with his national origin? The Bible says that it is *"the people"* of the prince that destroy Jerusalem. That is our clue! When was Jerusalem destroyed? 70 AD. Who destroyed it? Romans. One way or another the Antichrist is tied very closely to Rome.

Out of the TV screens and radios a voice proclaims, "My beloved children of god, my heart goes out to all of you that have experienced some kind of loss or another in the traumatic events that occurred two days ago. I wish from the bottom of my heart that I had some kind of answer for what happened that tragic day. I know many of you lost people in the mass disappearance, and some of you lost loved ones in the many accidents that occurred thereafter.

I am a man of faith; I serve a god of faith. When I do not understand things, he tells me that I only need to have faith and do what I can today for the betterment of my fellow man. I am not a man of science; I am a man of faith, so if there is a scientific explanation for what transpired I would be at a loss to explain it.

Some say this is the Rapture that the Bible speaks of – but if that is the case why am I still here? Why are so many other holy men of god, pastors, bishops, and clergymen still here? Many of you believe in god, and yet you still stand here as do I, left with only the memory of those that suddenly vanished.

No, it was not the Rapture, for the word Rapture does not even occur in the Bible! Regardless, I am not here to try and explain what happened, for in doing so I would change nothing.

I am not just a man of faith, but also a man of peace. If the world ever needed peace it is now. If the world ever needed faith it is now! I implore you to find hope in faith, and to find faith in your god – whoever that god may be! We do not need petty disagreements at a time like this, we need hope and unity!

It is in light of this need for unity that the Roman Catholic Church opens its arms to others, looking for hope, under a new title: the World Catholic Church. We are not as concerned with minor petty differences as we are with the need to find rest, to find hope and peace, and most of all to find love in a united world faith!

We will be opening the windows of Heaven upon the world. We have been blessed, and now we shall bless the world in her most desperate hour. There will be food donations, shelters, free medical care. You will be cared for, and you will find rest. Thank-you and may God bless you all."

Basically, while the whole world is going mad, he seems to be the only beacon of hope. This causes him to gain more and more power, until he is able to sign a covenant with the nation of Israel and many other nations. The covenant officially starts the seven year Tribulation (Dan. 9:27).

The Second Seal opens and a red horseman comes blazing out of it with a great sword drawn. This horseman gallops across the Earth spreading war everywhere he goes. Jesus said in *Matthew 24:6, "And ye shall hear of wars and rumours of wars: see that ye be not troubled: for all these things must come to pass, but the end is not yet."*

It is somewhat likely that around this time Israel turns to the Antichrist for help against a great threat from the north: the Russian Empire. Prophesies in Ezekiel 38 and 39 show Russia (along with many other Arab nations) at some point early one trying to annihilate the Jews, and without a doubt there are rumblings of war against Israel at this time. The Antichrist uses all the wars worldwide to further solidify his power.

The first and second horsemen run throughout the Earth simultaneously. One causes war and the other uses the message of peace and safety to conquer and subdue nations unto him. The covenant "with many" is signed, and we know the temple is rebuilt because the Antichrist allows the Israelites to resume animal sacrifices (Dan. 9:27).

Out of **the Third Seal** comes the third horseman on a Black Horse. Following on the heels of the Red Horse this one causes famine everywhere he goes. We are still in the first half of the Tribulation at this point and the Antichrist is continuing to gain more and more power.

People are starving, and oil is in short supply. Food is overpriced, and families begin to rely on the coalition of the Antichrist to ration out food to them. He unites the world in a socialist form to meet the needs of everyone. He takes food from the North American continent and feeds the world and in turn he uses Middle Eastern oil to meet the needs of the West and China.

Whether they like it or not, the world is now at the mercy of the Antichrist. Many nations are happy to throw their sovereignty in the pot to be a help to everyone and especially themselves. Others feel they have no choice at this time.

VI. The Middle Seal

The Fourth Seal opens, out comes the Pale Horse and everything changes dramatically. Death rides the horse, and Hell follows it. This is the point at which the Antichrist breaks the covenant with Israel.* The term "Death and Hell," used here to describe the Fourth Seal, ties in directly with Isaiah 28 in which the Jews form a covenant and then have it broken.

Isaiah 28:14-15, "Wherefore hear the word of the LORD, ye scornful men, that rule this people which is in Jerusalem. Because ye have said, We have made a covenant with <u>death, and with hell</u> are we at agreement; when the overflowing scourge shall pass through, it shall not come unto us: for we have made lies our refuge, and under falsehood have we hid ourselves:"

[*No where in the Bible does it say how many days there are between the Rapture and the start of the

Tribulation, the best indication is seventy-five days. There are seventy-five days from the end of the Tribulation to the beginning of the Millennium. There is more information on that in chapter seven.]

Israel knows that she should stay away from this man, but the passage says they make lies their refuge, trusting in him for protection. This covenant is with *"death and Hell."*

Isaiah 28:18, "And your <u>covenant with death</u> shall be disannulled, and your <u>agreement with hell</u> shall not stand; when the overflowing scourge shall pass through, then ye shall be trodden down by it."

God uses Isaiah to prophesy that this covenant that Israel forms for protection will not stand and that the "overflowing scourge" is unavoidable.

For quick recap:

1. We have Daniel saying that the Antichrist forms a covenant with Israel (and others as well) that will last one week (seven years) and that the Antichrist breaks this covenant in the middle of the week (the three and a half year mark). Dan. 9:27

2. Isaiah calls this the covenant with Death and Hell and says it will not stand, and that trouble is unavoidable. Is. 28:14-15, 18

3. The Fourth Seal (no coincidence it's the middle seal out of the seven) opens in Rev. 6:7-8 and out comes Death and Hell with the Pale Horse, clearly marking the breaking of the covenant and the middle of the Tribulation.

As the Pale Horse crosses the Earth he destroys a quarter of the population with hunger, the beasts of the Earth, death and the sword. Before this time animals feared man, but now they see man as prey. Widespread famine and disease are rampant.

Death by the sword represents more war. There is good evidence for a specific war that is found in Ez. 38-39 to occur around this time.

VII. The War of Ezekiel 38 and 39

In Ezekiel 38 and 39 there is a prophecy about the land of Gog and Magog and the cities of Meshech and Tubal invading Israel. Gog and Magog refer to the modern day land of Russia, and Meshech and Tubal are what we know today to be Moscow and Tobolsk.

As of 2010, this prophesied battle still hasn't occurred. It can't happen before the Tribulation or right at the beginning of it, because in Ez. 38:11 the enemy says that he is going to invade Israel when they least expect it: *"...I will go up to the land of __unwalled villages__; I will go to them that are at rest, that __dwell safely__, all of them dwelling without walls, and having neither bars nor gates..."*

Constant terror attack and threats from neighboring Arab states make it impossible for Israel to be at rest now or at the beginning of the Tribulation. It also can't be Armageddon because towards the end of the Tribulation they are running for their lives and expect danger then as well.

There really is little chance that it could be the battle of Gog and Magog later on at the end of the Millennium. In Gog and Magog, the Devil is the leader and the whole world comes to attack a single city: Jerusalem. Additionally, right after they are defeated the Great White Throne Judgment occurs. Following that, God then destroys the Earth and makes a brand new heavens and Earth (Rev. 21-22). There simply isn't room for what the Bible says happens *after* the attack to occur.

In contrast, in Ezekiel 38 and 39 the attacker is Russia and many of her allies against a whole country (Ez. 38:1-7), some of the enemies still survive (39:2), and Israel spends seven months cleaning up the dead attacking army (Ez. 39:12). Among other differences, all the enemies get wiped out in Rev. 20, and there's no time for burying anyone afterwards. This is the reasoning for Ezekiel 38-39 occurring a little under a year before the middle of the Tribulation.

For a brief period of time the Antichrist was able to unite the world in a socialist coalition. *Daniel 8:25 says, "And through his policy also __he shall cause craft to prosper__ in his hand..."* This peace didn't last long, but it did last long enough for Israel to let their guard down. A plausible scenario is as follows:

Russia, Libya, Ethiopia, and many other nations descend upon Israel before they know what hit them. The goal of the invading army is annihilation. Fighters, bombers and missiles fill the air as ground troops make ready for invasion and mop-up action.

Israel does the best they can to defend their little country, but before they can get a plane off the ground, torrential rain and giant hailstones begin falling from the sky. The stones fall as though they were cast from heavens, taking out any and all threats in the air. Bombs explode high enough to where they can't do any damage to the people below, and the wreckage falls in between buildings and in open spaces. No Jew is hurt; the warm rain melts the hail enough to where it squishes on the ground like a snow cone in summer.

The Russian alliance is furious and sends in their ground forces, but before a shot can be fired, burning lava rocks and fire fall upon them. The brimstone is God's napalm, burning through any and all armored tanks that would destroy His people. Fire comes down from Heaven scorching the life out of the ground forces.

The Russian alliance is decimated. Between all of the nations that were bound together, only one-sixth of their total armed forces remain. The Arab states curse Russia and flee to their own lands fearing retaliation from Israel.

Back in the land of Palestine, a refreshing rain falls upon them as they praise Jehovah. They still do not see Jesus Christ as their Messiah.

The Antichrist and his coalition condemn this blatant attack and swear to their ally Israel that they will defend them. They invade many of these countries, subduing them to the will of the ten-nation alliance of Rome. At that point, in comes the Antichrist's peacekeeping force. Though hesitant to comply, Israel trusts the Antichrist because her old allies, the United States and England.

At some point in the middle of the Tribulation the Antichrist is assassinated (Rev. 13:3). Three days later he rises from the dead, indwelled by Satan, and becomes the Son of Perdition (II Thess. 2:3). At this point he breaks the covenant with the nation of Israel, stops the temple sacrifices and sits down in the Holy of Holies declaring himself to be God (Dan. 8:25, II Thess. 2:3-4). His ten-nation coalition crushes the Roman Church he used to get him into power (Rev. 17:16) which ensures that he shares his worship with no one.

VIII. From the Martyrs to the Advent

In comes **the Fifth Seal.** As soon as the Jews see their sovereignty ripped from them and the Antichrist demanding worship from the Mercy Seat, they start running. If there is one thing any Jew knows it's that you don't worship an image, and when the image starts speaking and demanding worship they literally run for the hills (Matt. 24:15-20). They flee to the rock of Petra and are fed by God with manna (Lam. 5:9, Is. 26:20; 42:11-12). Millions are captured or slain by the Antichrist's forces.

II Thessalonians 2:3-4, "Let no man deceive you by any means: for that day shall not come, except there come a falling away first, and that man of sin be revealed, the son of perdition; Who opposeth and exalteth himself above all that is called God, or that is worshipped; so that <u>he as God sitteth in the temple of God, shewing himself that he is God.</u>"

The Antichrist, the False Prophet, and the Image of the Beast bring in the mark. All people from every nation are commanded to take the mark of allegiance to the Beast. Any that refuse the mark cannot buy, sell or live – they are beheaded. Some refuse to take this mark, both Jew and Gentile. The sides are clearly drawn as Moses and Elijah have arrived on Earth testifying of the Gospel of the Kingdom and denouncing the Antichrist.

The mark spreads throughout the world, propelled by the religious signs of the Beast and the False Prophet. It is accepted unconditionally at first, but there is internal war within the empire of the Beast (Dan. 11:40-44) before Christ comes back. Towards the end of the Tribulation the Antichrist begins losing his grasp on the world (Dan. 11:41).

Towards the end of the Tribulation the Antichrist has a massive army, part of it containing 200 million demonic horsemen (Rev. 9:16-19). The Antichrist moves the most powerful army ever assembled to fight God Himself in the Valley of Megiddo.

In comes **the Sixth Seal**. When comparing the Sixth Seal to Christ returning in Matt. 24:29-30 you'll see it's the same thing. The sun becomes black and virtually disappears as the moon turns a dark bloody crimson color. Stars (meteorites or maybe angels, see Rev. 1:20) start falling from the sky as the ground begins to quake. The armies look into the sky to see what is happening. What they see is called the sign of the Son of Man. This is what we see occurring in the Sixth Seal, the moments right before Armageddon.

As the armies see the sign, they know that an angel, or God or something supernatural is coming for them.

There are many things in Revelation 6:12-17 that clearly point to this being the moment right before Christ comes back. It speaks of kings, mighty men and chief captains running and hiding from the *"wrath of the Lamb"* and from *"the face of him that sitteth on the throne."* They see Christ's face and run! The final remark concerning the Sixth Seal is *"For the great day of his wrath is come; and who shall be able to stand?"*

Now, to come to **the Seventh Seal** we have to skip past all of Revelation 7 and go to Revelation 8:1. We'll soon see that Revelation 7 is parenthetical and doesn't follow the natural order of events in this account.

Rev. 8:1, "And when he had opened the seventh seal, there was <u>silence in heaven</u> about the space of half an hour."

What is the Seventh Seal? What is that silence in Heaven for the space of a half hour? Maybe it's silent in Heaven because the Sixth Seal is Armageddon and everyone is at the battle! Does everyone in Heaven join in the fray? Is Heaven empty and that's why it's quiet?

Whether or not Heaven is empty, the Seventh Seal is the moment Christ obtains His kingdom and that is the reason why there is silence in Heaven for an half hour.

Zechariah 2:10-13, "Sing and rejoice, O daughter of Zion: for, lo, I come, and <u>I will dwell in the midst</u>

of thee, saith the LORD. And many nations shall be joined to the LORD in that day, and shall be my people: and I will dwell in the midst of thee, and thou shalt know that the LORD of hosts hath sent me unto thee. And the <u>LORD shall inherit Judah his portion in the holy land</u>, and shall choose Jerusalem again. <u>Be silent, O all flesh, before the LORD</u>: for he is raised up out of his holy habitation."

We see Calvary as the greatest day of all because our sins were paid for, but God the Father sees the day His Son comes into glory as a greater day. God is far more interested in the day that His Son gains the kingdom prophesied throughout the entire Bible than the day He was cruelly beaten and crucified! Not only is all of Heaven silent at this time, but all flesh will be silent as well.

IX. What about Chapter Seven?

Chapter seven* starts out with 144,000 Jews being sealed with the seal of God in their foreheads. The sealing of the 144,000 Jews probably happens before any of the seals in Revelation are opened. The reason for this is because during the Seals the Earth is being hurt, except for maybe the first seal. This is significant because in Rev. 7:3 an angel says *not to hurt the Earth* until the servants of God are sealed. Famine, crops and food destroyed all equate to the Earth being hurt. During wars the Earth is always hurt as well. All this occurs *after* the sealing of the 144,000.

Not only are the 144,000 sealed *before* these Seals come to pass, but we'll see later they are also raptured out during the middle of the Tribulation.

[*This chapter is parenthetical, which essentially means that it is interjected in the middle of something (in this case the Seals), and doesn't necessarily fit the flow of what you just read. Basically, it's a break from what you were reading and a look at something else. This break occurs right before the Seventh Seal, and the same thing will happen in the second account right before the Seventh Trumpet.]

The 144,000 consist of twelve thousand Jewish male virgins sealed here from twelve tribes of Israel (don't let someone tell you otherwise; Revelation 7 is clear on this). **Throughout the Old Testament the tribes of the children of Israel were as follows:**

1. Reuben
2. Simeon
3. Judah
4. Zebulun
5. Issachar
6. Dan
7. Gad
8. Asher
9. Naphtali
10. Ephraim
11. Manasseh (Sometimes "the half tribe of...")
12. Benjamin

Levi (Levi was the priestly tribe and was not counted as one of the twelve).

Here are the twelve tribes mentioned in Rev. 7:
1. Juda
2. Reuben
3. Gad
4. Aser
5. Nepthalim
6. Manases*
7. Simeon
8. Levi
9. Issachar
10. Zabulon
11. Joseph
12. Benjamin

Dan is gone! In its place you have the tribe of Levi (Ephraim was the son of Joseph so there is no real significance to the name change there). The reason for this is because Dan got into trouble with idol worship to the point that he was cut out of God's program and replaced (Judges 17-18).

[*Some spellings here in English may differ from the Old Testament readings because in Greek they are spelled differently than they are in Hebrew. Then in turn when you translate them from Greek to English the spelling varies as well. This is an example of the King James Bible's superiority to other English versions which vary from the Greek to try and make the spelling the same in English as you would find in the Old Testament. This is an example of one of the many liberties that the translators of modern versions take in new versions that are published every year – they tweak them to their own likings instead of staying accurate.]

In *Revelation 7:9-10* it says, *"After this I beheld, and, lo, a great multitude, <u>which no man could number</u>, <u>of all nations</u>, and kindreds, and people, and tongues, stood before the throne, and before the Lamb, clothed with white robes, and palms in their hands; And cried with a loud voice, saying, Salvation to our God which sitteth upon the throne, and unto the Lamb."*

After seeing the 144,000 sealed and prepared to go out and preach through the first three and a half years of the Tribulation, John's vision jumps forward and in Revelation 7:9-10 he sees the martyrs of the second half of the Tribulation. Many of these were led to the Lord by the 144,000 he had just seen get ready to go out to preach (visions are strange like that). As Paul was *"one born out of due time"* (a Jew preaching the gospel to the Gentiles), so these 144,000 Jews will evangelize the world for Christ.

All these in Revelation 7:9-10 are those that have come out of *"great tribulation"* through martyrdom. The Great Tribulation is the second half of the Tribulation that Jesus talks about in Matthew 24 when He specifically uses the term *"great tribulation."* It is wonderful to see that it is a *"great multitude"* that *"no man could number"** that refuse to take the mark!

They stand in the face of opposition, certain death; they refuse to take the mark. Like the three Hebrew children that would not bow to Nebuchadnezzar, these

59

brave souls to come will refuse to bow to an image, a man or a mark. History has seemed to show that the greatest persecution brings about the greatest heroes for Christ and it will show that again.

[*In spite of this very clear passage, many balk at the idea that there will be a great multitude saved in the Tribulation, mostly because of the common misconception that people who hear the gospel now can't get saved after the Rapture. The Bible never says this, anywhere. What it does say, is that after the Wicked One has been revealed and the Man of Sin sits in the Temple of God, that God will send a strong delusion to those who have rejected the gospel. This happens in the middle of the Tribulation, not the beginning of it. I Thess. 2]

In verses thirteen through seventeen, as John looks upon this vast sea of white-robed Tribulation saints, one of the elders humorously asks him who these people are and where they came from. John, amazed, overwhelmed and probably a little confused by the whole scene, quickly blurts out, *"Sir, thou knowest."*

The elder then describes to him what we read in the last verses of chapter seven. He describes people who are no longer hurting, scared, and hungry. He sees people that have finally found peace.

Well, there you have it: we finished the first road. If it was a little bumpy and if there were some parts that weren't entirely clear to you, that's fine. Remember, the Seals are an overview of the whole Tribulation and therefore don't focus on some of the other aspects that the other "streets" will. If things are fuzzy, they will become clearer as we look at the three accounts to come. The two witnesses, Babylon, the mid-Trib and post-Trib Raptures... these and other landmarks are all things we'll find on the roads to come.

CHAPTER FOUR

WITNESS WAY

"Then said he, These are the two
anointed ones, that stand by the
Lord of the whole earth."
Zechariah 4:14

THE SECOND ACCOUNT
Revelation 8:2-11:19

THE SEVEN TRUMPETS & THREE WOES

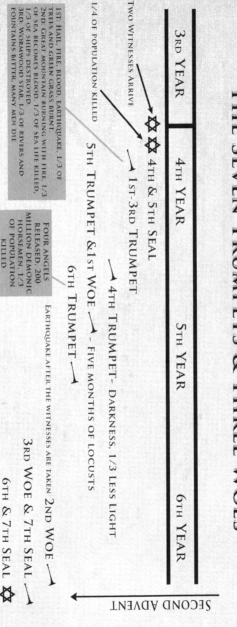

| 3RD YEAR | 4TH YEAR | 5TH YEAR | 6TH YEAR |

TWO WITNESSES ARRIVE

1/4 OF POPULATION KILLED

4TH & 5TH SEAL

1ST-3RD TRUMPET

1ST HAIL, FIRE, BLOOD, EARTHQUAKE. 1/3 OF TREES AND GREEN GRASS BURNT 2ND- GREAT MOUNTAIN BURNING WITH FIRE, 1/3 OF SEA BECOMES BLOOD, 1/3 OF SEA LIFE KILLED, 1/3 OF SHIPS DESTROYED 3RD- WORMWOOD STAR, 1/3 OF RIVERS AND FOUNTAINS BITTER, MANY MEN DIE

5TH TRUMPET &1ST WOE

4TH TRUMPET- DARKNESS. 1/3 LESS LIGHT

6TH TRUMPET

FOUR ANGELS RELEASED, 200 MILLION DEMONIC HORSEMEN, 1/3 OF POPULATION KILLED

EARTHQUAKE AFTER THE WITNESSES ARE TAKEN 2ND WOE

- FIVE MONTHS OF LOCUSTS

3RD WOE & 7TH SEAL

6TH & 7TH SEAL

= BEGINNING OF TRUMPET AND/OR WOE

= BEGINNING OF SEAL

SECOND ADVENT

I. The Arrival of the Witnesses

As the Antichrist raised his fist towards Heaven mocking God, two men entered the temple and stood near the golden candlestick. Neither one of these men looked like they belonged in this century. The taller one had white hair, a white beard, wore a robe and held a staff in his right hand. The other man was dressed unusually as well: he had on some kind of leather garment covered with coarse hair, and there was a three-inch-thick strap of leather around his waist.

The moment these men appeared, the cameras turned from recording the man on the Mercy Seat and towards the two strangers. Without hesitation, the old gray-haired man raised his hand in the air and said, "Thus saith the Lord, Thou shalt not have any gods before Me, and thou shalt not make unto thee any graven image!"

The man clothed in camel's hair added, "You have three and a half years, and then you'll be cut off! And in the meantime, the only rain you'll get is hail, fire and blood!"

Finally coming to their senses, the temple soldiers who had just seen everything unfold rushed toward the two witnesses. As they came at the two men, Moses and Elijah looked at them and opened their mouths as if to speak. Only instead of words coming out of their mouths, out came fire and incinerated the troops immediately.

Powerless to do anything, the man on the Mercy Seat could only sit and watch while these two men made *a mockery of his power. Turning to face the Son of Perdition, Elijah said, "Is this the man that made the nations tremble? Thou shalt be brought down to Hell, to the sides of the pit!"*

With that the two walked out the door of the temple and addressed the crowd outside with these words:

"Hear the word of the Lord of Israel, when ye therefore shall see the abomination of desolation, spoken of by Daniel the prophet, stand in the Holy Place, then let them which be in Judaea flee into the mountains: For then shall be Great Tribulation, such as was not since the beginning of the world to this time, no, nor ever shall be!"

The next account of Christ's Second Coming covers the Trumpet plagues and the actions of the two witnesses. As the Seals were an overview of the whole seven years, this account focuses on the continual bombardment that God brings down on the kingdom of the Antichrist.

To get a good grasp of this account and how it fits in with the Seals, we need to know when the Trumpets begin and when the two witnesses arrive.

II. Where Do the Trumpets Start?

At this point in our study we should have a good idea of the Seals. We should know the first one starts with the rise of the Antichrist, the middle Seal of Death and Hell marks the middle of the Tribulation, and the Sixth and Seventh Seals represent the end.

The Seventh Seal has two elements to it. It has the **chronological layer** of it actually being the Second Advent, and the **narrative element** in which it is "the calm before the storm." Basically, John saw the whole vision all at one time and part of that was the silent awe in Heaven before the Trumpets entered the scene. This calm before the storm is the reason why God put it as the first verse in chapter eight. This silence shows the fear and reverence for what is about to happen. God is about to pour out His wrath like never before on Earth.

That still doesn't answer the question of when the First Trumpet starts.

Revelation 8:3-4, "And another angel came and stood at the altar, having a golden censer; and there was given unto him much incense, that he should offer it with <u>the prayers of all saints</u> upon the golden altar which was before the throne. And <u>the smoke of the incense, which came with the prayers of the saints</u>, ascended up before God out of the angel's hand."

Before the Trumpets sound, it is the prayers of the martyrs that ascend up to God. This is what we see in the Fifth Seal! If you look at Rev. 6:9-11 you see these martyred souls under an altar crying up to God for vengeance. The vengeance they're crying for is *not* the Trumpet judgments; they want Jesus to remove the Antichrist from his seat of power.

God tells these martyrs that they have to wait, but we see the rest of the story here. God hears their prayers and starts pouring out wrath. These Trumpets occur right about the time of the Fifth Seal. If you remember, the Fourth Seal is right in the middle of the Tribulation. We'll see more clearly as we go on that this is when the mark is introduced, and with the mark comes the martyrs that refuse it. Therefore, the Trumpets start right around the middle of the Tribuation, probably a few months after.

Now that we've placed the start of the Trumpets, we need to jump clear past the Trumpets to chapter eleven and see when the two witnesses arrive.

III. When Do the Two Witnesses Arrive?

Revelation 11:3-5, "And I will give power unto my two witnesses, and <u>they shall prophesy a thousand two hundred and threescore days</u>, clothed in sackcloth. These are the two olive trees, and the two candlesticks standing before the God of the earth. And if any man will hurt them, fire proceedeth out of their mouth, and devoureth their enemies: and if any man will hurt them, he must in this manner be killed."

God sends His two witnesses down to Earth right in the middle of the Tribulation. We can know this for sure because it says they prophesy for *"a thousand two hundred and threescore days,"* which is three and a half years (a "score" in the Bible is the number twenty). Furthermore, the events following their deaths and ascensions are right at the end of the Tribulation.

Revelation 11:12-15, "And they heard a great voice from heaven saying unto them, <u>Come up</u>

hither. And they ascended up to heaven in a cloud; and their enemies beheld them. And the same hour was there a great earthquake, and the tenth part of the city fell, and in the earthquake were slain of men seven thousand: and the remnant were affrighted, and gave glory to the God of heaven. The second woe is past; and, behold, the third woe cometh quickly. And the seventh angel sounded; and there were great voices in heaven, saying, The kingdoms of this world are become the kingdoms of our Lord, and of his Christ; and he shall reign for ever and ever."

As you can see, it says in the same hour there was a great earthquake and right after that the kingdoms of this world become Jesus Christ's kingdom. This shows us that two witnesses show up in the middle and are present for three and half years; they are then killed and ascend to Heaven after three days, and shortly thereafter Armageddon takes place. If you want to be exact, the best place to put the witnesses is arriving three days before the middle of the Tribulation.

IV. Who Are the Two Witnesses?

The two witnesses are none other than *Moses and Elijah the prophet.* When Moses was on the Earth, God used him to turn water to blood and to smite the land of Egypt with plagues. Part of that was destroying people with fire (Ex. 9:23-24). Elijah caused it to not rain in the land of Israel for three years under the reign of Ahab (I Kings 17:1). These are the same things that these two witnesses will be doing during the Tribulation.

Revelation 11:6, "These have power to shut heaven, <u>that it rain not</u> in the days of their prophecy: and have power over waters to turn them to blood, and <u>to smite the earth with all plagues</u>, as often as they will."

It is also interesting to note that it was Moses and Elijah that appeared with Jesus on the Mount of Transfiguration. There is ample evidence for the two witnesses being Moses and Elijah when you start comparing the things that they both did and the places they were. Consider the fact that they both went without food or water, and they did it on the same mountain (Sinai is a summit of Mt. Horeb. Ex. 34:28-29, I Kings 19:8)!

When John the Baptist showed up at Christ's First Coming, he was prophesied to come in the "spirit and power" of Elijah (Luke 1:17). At the same time, Christ said John would have actually been Elijah *(that's an example of believing something that you may not quite understand)* if Israel had received the Gospel of the kingdom. It was said that John the Baptist could have been Elijah because there is prophecy about Elijah coming back before the Messiah comes. They didn't accept Christ as their Messiah, so he wasn't. There could be a whole other book on what would have happened if they had accepted Him!

Malachi 4:4-5, "Remember <u>ye the law of Moses my servant</u>, which I commanded unto him in Horeb for all Israel, with the statutes and judgments.

69

*Behold, **I will send you Elijah the prophet** before the coming of the great and dreadful day of the LORD:"*

It is also interesting to note that Moses is mentioned in the prophecy of Elijah coming back. For the most part, when the Bible talks about "the day of the LORD" in the Old Testament, it is speaking of Armageddon and the millennial reign of Christ. This is why you'll read passages that talk about the day being terrible, dark, and wonderful at the same time. Elijah is supposed to return before the day of the Lord.

Did you ever stop to consider why Moses never showed signs of slowing down from old age? How many eighty year old men have you ever seen that can storm up and down mountains like Moses did? The Bible says that when Moses died, at 120 years old, he was very cognizant and in great health. *"...his eye was not dim, nor his natural force abated."* in *Duet 34:7*. The next thing you know Michael the Archangel and Satan are arguing about the body of Moses in Jude 9. Why would that be? What a strange thing!

While you're considering that, think about Elijah. The man spent his life walking all over the place, hiding in caves, and there's even an instance where once the spirit of God came over Elijah he outran a chariot. He was in excellent health his whole life, just like Moses, and when God took him to Heaven he was still in great shape.

God kept both men in great physical conditioning because one day they were going to need to use their bodies again, down here on Earth. When Moses died his spirit returned to the father (all human spirits do), his soul went to Paradise (in the middle of the Earth at the time), and his body went to the ground. However something different happened with Moses' body. Shortly after Moses died Michael took his body up to Heaven before it saw corruption, so that it could be used again. Elijah went to Heaven in his natural body and will return in the same body.

Why will both of them use their old bodies over again, why not a new one? Because a glorified body can't die, and both of these men will have to die when they come back.

There are many other ideas about who the two witnesses are, but there really isn't a lot of evidence to support them. Some of the ideas are that they could be just a couple of Jews out of the middle of nowhere, or one of them could be Enoch.

The evidence for one of the two witnesses being Enoch is that Enoch never died and *"...it is appointed unto men once to die..."* That is pretty much where the evidence begins and ends. While it's true that death is appointed, that doesn't mean it's going to happen. *There's going to be a lot of people that are going to get out of that appointment!*

Hebrews 11:5, "By faith Enoch was translated that he should not see death; and <u>was not found</u>, because God had translated him: for before his translation he had this testimony, that he pleased God."

Enoch avoided death, and he's a picture of the church getting raptured out before the Tribulation.

We avoid the Tribulation; Enoch avoided the flood. Saying someone is "appointed" for death isn't a guarantee that they will in fact die, otherwise the doctrine of the rapture would simply fall apart. When the Bible says Enoch isn't going to *see* death, it means in the future as well.

V. Back to the Trumpets

Two weeks have passes since the prophets delivered their message to the people of Israel. Thousands have been killed daily while trying to flee the control of the Antichrist. The two prophets have been preaching in the streets nonstop to the people that their Messiah is coming. The two have been demonstrating with signs and wonders the evidence of their message.

Inside the temple, the Son of Perdition sits, accepting worship. The doors swing open, and in walk the messengers of God.

"So very sorry to interrupt your worship service..." Elijah says in a mocking bow before the King of Fierce Countenance.

The hand of Moses goes up in the air and his voice thunders, "Thus saith the Lord, I will bring again the captivity of my people of Israel! What mean ye that ye beat my people to pieces, and grind the faces of the poor? Let my people go!"

"Or what?!" screams the demon-possessed man. Without hesitation, the two turn and walk right back out where they came from. As they pass the altar in the courtyard, Moses and Elijah both raise their rods in the

air. At that moment hail, fire, and blood comes raining out of the sky and worldwide upon the empire of the Beast.

The Bible doesn't say they're the ones making all this happen, but it wouldn't be a surprise. The Bible does say in **Ecclesiastes 1:9, "The thing that hath been, it is that which shall be; and <u>that which is done is that which shall be done</u>: and there is no new thing under the sun."**

In comes the **First Trumpet** judgment (Rev. 8:7) of hail, fire and blood. At this point one-third of the trees on the Earth are burnt up along with all the grass. This corresponds to the seventh plague of Egypt (Ex. 9:18-26).

Shortly thereafter, the **Second Trumpet** comes to pass with one-third of the sea life being killed and a third of the ships destroyed. A burning mountain falls from the sky and turns another third of the sea to blood. This corresponds to the first plague of Egypt (Ex.7:19-21).

Next comes the **Third Trumpet**, and with it a star falls from Heaven polluting a third of the rivers and fountains. This could be a meteorite, or it could be a fallen angel. Stars are sometimes angels in the Bible (Rev. 1:20). This star has a name: Wormwood.

We are now about to go on a little rabbit trail, but this is very important. The first time Christ came, *He preached the Gospel of the Kingdom* (Mt. 10:5-7). It was this gospel, or good news, that was for the Jews and had the signs associated with it.

The purpose of the Gospel of the Kingdom was to compel Israel to accept their Messiah as the Lamb of God first, then accept Him as their king (Jn. 1:29; Mt. 6:33). The people of Israel knew all the Old Testament prophesies about the glory of Israel and their Messiah reigning (Zech. 8:22-23; Is. 2:2-4). However, they wanted the blessings without the repentance, and they rejected Him.

Jesus, His disciples and His apostles used signs and miracles to convince the Jews (Mt. 10:5-7, 15:24, Jn. 2:23; 7:31, I Cor. 1:22; 14:22). This is the reason the signs began to wane throughout the book of Acts, with Paul unable to heal himself or his friends (II Tim. 4:11, II Tim. 4:20, I Tim. 5:23). As it became more and more apparent that Israel was not going to repent, the gospel went to the Gentile (Acts 7; 13:46-48; 18:5-6; 28:27-28).

The point is this: it's important to understand that during the Tribulation God's attention is once again back towards Israel! When that happens, *there is a resurgence of the Gospel of the Kingdom* (Mt. 24:14) and all the signs and wonders that came with it the first time. People are preaching that the kingdom is right around the corner and the Messiah will arrive shortly! In this Third Trumpet we have water being poisoned and people dying from it. Those that have accepted Christ will not die from drinking the poisoned water, just like they didn't during the Apostolic Age.

If you remember, the Fourth Seal (the one that marks the middle of the Tribulation) is the one in which a fourth of the Earth is killed. People die in both the Fourth and Fifth Seal. The difference is that the Fifth Seal focuses on the martyrs. The Fourth Seal doesn't stop with the beginning of the Fifth Seal, because the Fifth Seal is pretty much right on top of the Fourth. In other words, the Fourth Seal continues through the Fifth.

The First, Second and Third Trumpets happen at the same time as the Fourth and Fifth Seals. This is evident because a fourth of the Earth's population is killed in both accounts. As of the time of this writing, we have over six billion people on Earth, so that would mean in the space of about a year one and a half billion people die on Earth.

In comes **the Fourth Trumpet.** A third of the sun, moon and stars are darkened. In Mk. 13:20, it says God in His mercy and for the sake of His people *"hath shortened the days"* in reference to the Tribulation. With the days being shorter, things move faster. The last half of the seven year Tribulation is the worst half, and so far in this account we've been actually looking at the first half of the last half.

The Earth becomes darker as the judgment of God intensifies. The next two Trumpets are also Woes, and the final Trumpet immediately follows the final Woe.

Now is time for **the Fifth Trumpet and First Woe.** We are now entering the last two years of the Tribulation. The way you can tell is by looking at the length of the next two Trumpets. In this Fifth Trumpet the locusts are on the Earth five months. Now if you jump ahead and look at Rev. 9:15, the Sixth Trumpet lasts one year, one month, one day, and one hour. Those two together are about a year and a half of time.

We will see in chapter six that the Vials will take about six months before the end, and that they take place in between the Sixth and Seventh Trumpets. When the seventh angel sounds the Seventh Trumpet, (Rev. 10:6-7; 11:15) it's all over for the Antichrist. That gives us a time frame of roughly two years left at the start of the Fifth Trumpet.

The **Fifth Trumpet** opens with a star falling from Heaven. This star is the king over the Bottomless Pit, and he is allowed to open the pit. This star is Satan.

As Satan opens the pit, the air fills with small flying creatures. The sun is darkened by the smoke that arises out of the pit. These creatures are the size of locusts, but they are shaped like horses. They have the faces of men, wear crowns, have long hair, and are armored. Not exactly something your local *Orkin man* is used to dealing ith.

These demonic things have scorpion-like stingers, and they use them to torment men for five months. The pain is so excruciating that *men want to die*, but can't. Satan is their king; he is Apollyon, Abaddon, and the Destroyer. These creatures aren't planes, jets or some other kind of flying devices. If they were, they wouldn't have the Devil over them and the whole long-hair-face-like-men-teeth-like-lions-coming-out-of-the-bottomless-pit thing wouldn't fit all that well either.

They are only allowed by God to torment those who do not have the seal of God in their foreheads. At first it appears that it's only the 144,000, but maybe when someone gets saved in the Tribulation they are marked of God. The direct converts of the twelve apostles received the apostolic signs; perhaps in the Tribulation the direct converts of the 144,000 receive the seal of God in their foreheads as well.

We are getting closer to the end, and now we see the **Sixth Trumpet** come to pass. Four fallen angels are released from their prison (Jude 6-7, I Peter 3:19-20), and we see the emergence of a satanic, 200-million-man army. This army is on horseback and rides fire-breathing horses that have lion heads. The tails of these beasts are like snakes, they have literal heads on them that inflict pain. This army roams the Earth for over a year slaughtering unrepentant idolaters.

The population of Earth is cut down another third by these hordes. The Fourth and Fifth Seals *and* First through Third Trumpets combine to cut an Earth of six billion down to four and a half billion, and this army cuts it down by another one and a half billion, down to a remaining three billion. At least half of the world's population is dead now. When you take into account the missing Church Age saints, worldwide war, famine, and the general overall madness of the Tribulation, you could reasonably estimate another one billion gone. That leaves you a world of two billion with a year and a half to go.

Right about now we are nearing the end. Just like Revelation seven was parenthetical, so too is chapter ten. So for now we'll skip past Rev. 10 and rejoin the actions of the two witnesses in Rev. 11:7.

VI. The Grand Finale

It's been well over three years since the two prophets first appeared in Israel. Since then, the holocaust carried out against their followers has been devastating. The Jewish race has been cut down from millions to only several thousand hiding out. Part of the Remnant live within an Underground Railroad system and another part live within the rock city of Petra. God has protected those living within the rock and has fed them at night with manna.

The testimony of the two prophets is coming to a close. At this point the vast majority of people have chosen sides. Much of the preaching lately has been similar to the preaching of the angel: fear God, give Him glory, and reject the mark because He's coming back very soon. This comes as a terrible message of condemnation to most.

The Scripture poured out of Elijah's mouth as the army surrounded him and Moses. "If any man worship the Beast and his image, and receive his mark in his forehead, or in his hand, the same shall drink of the wine of the wrath of God..."

They stood alone upon a hill. The last two groups of soldiers that tried to apprehend them that day were burnt alive by fire coming down from Heaven. This time was different though, the leader of this group realized that angering them wasn't going to help his plans any. Though he was a worshipper of the Beast, he feared God and didn't want to die today.

The soldiers stopped at the command of their leader. At their feet lay the blackened and charred remains of the last two groups that tried what they were about to try. They didn't take another step.

Laying down his weapons, he approached the two men with his hands in the air. "Please, sirs, I didn't ask for these orders, but I've been told to arrest you. I'm asking you that maybe my life and the lives of these men could be precious in your sight and you would come along with us peaceably?"

With that they did.

"Thus saith the Lord, Woe to the bloody city..." The voice of Moses rang out over the crowd as they slipped the mask over the face of Elijah.

"...Therefore I will judge you, O house of Israel, every one according to his ways, saith the Lord GOD. Repent, and turn yourselves..." Elijah was now on his knees with his head on the block.

"Thus saith the Lord..." The blood-stained axe was lifted in the air.

"...destroy this temple, and in three days I will raise it up!"

After three days of lying in the streets of Jerusalem, the lifeless bodies of the two witnesses will come to life. The wicked who rejoiced over their death will be filled with fear. A great voice will come out from Heaven, *"Come up hither."* And they'll be taken straight up in a cloud right in front of their enemies. Just like when Jesus rose from the dead (Mt. 28:2), there will be an earthquake here as well. This earthquake is the **Second Woe**. Seven thousand people die in the earthquake and one-tenth of Jerusalem is destroyed. At this point, it says that the Third Woe is coming up quickly.

Chronologically speaking, **Revelation ten** now unfolds. As we saw earlier, chapter ten is parenthetical and as such it is somewhat independent from the rest of the account. In chapter ten we see the Mighty Angel and His interaction with John. This Mighty Angel is Jesus Christ, He roars like the Lion of the Tribe of Judah. This Angel is still talking in the beginning of chapter eleven, and he refers to the two witnesses as *"my two witnesses."* Only Christ would refer to them as such.

This is the Angel of the Lord appearing before Christ comes back to Earth. This is similar to a Theophany (or sometimes called a Christophany, both of which are an appearance of the Lord in the Old Testament). Moses, Joshua and many other Old Testament men *saw* a physical *appearance* of God *before* Jesus was born. The Angel speaks up to verse fourteen, and then *He* blows the Trumpet in verse fifteen, therefore the timing for this event is right beore the Seventh Trumpet.

When the **Seventh Trumpet** sounds, Jesus Christ is king.* **The Third Woe** then is Armageddon, which *comes* before the Seventh Trumpet sounding.

Revelation 11:14-15, "The second woe is past; and, behold, the third woe cometh quickly. And the seventh angel sounded; and there were great voices

in heaven, saying, <u>The kingdoms of this world are</u>
<u>become the kingdoms of our Lord, and of his</u>
<u>Christ; and he shall reign for ever and ever.</u>"

This is where the account ends. What follows this
is a remarkable prophecy within a prophecy! The text
in verses seventeen and eighteen is what the twenty-
four elders say up in Heaven at the point of Christ
becoming king. In verse seventeen they praise Him,
but in verse eighteen they speak of things to take place
later.

[*The "pre-wrath" rapture argument teaches that
the church is raptured out in the middle of the
Tribulation, before the wrath of God is poured out on
the Earth. As already stated, this theory ignores the
wrath of God in the first half. The only real evidence
for this idea is I Cor. 15:52 which refers to us being
raptured out at the "last trump." The pre-wrath
argument claims that we are raptured out at the
Seventh Trumpet in Revelation – which would be this
one.

The problem is the last Trumpet in Revelation is at
the very end of the Tribulation, meaning that if we're
raptured out at that point we go through all of the
wrath of God. The solution is found in the Old
Testament, specifically in Numbers 10, where trumpets
were used to move the camp or to give orders. This is
what Paul is referring to. The "last trump" is simply
God's final command to the church on Earth: "come up
hither."]

ROADMAP THROUGH REVELATION

VII. Prophecies within Prophecies

Revelation 11:18, "And the nations were angry, and thy wrath is come..."

The "wrath" that *follows* Armageddon is either the Judgment of the Nations in Mt. 25:31-46, or more likely the battle of Gog and Magog in Rev. 20:7-9. No one is going to be *angry* right after Christ destroys about a quarter of a billion armed soldiers and takes over the Earth as ruler: maybe terrified, but not angry. So it seems to be the battle of Gog and Magog.

"...and the time of the dead, that they should be judged, and that thou shouldest give reward unto thy servants the prophets, and to the saints, and them that fear thy name, small and great; and shouldest destroy them which destroy the earth."

The judgment that follows Gog and Magog is the Great White Throne Judgment. We'll see later that this is the one in which men are judged according to their works, and if their names are not written down in the book of life they are thrown into the Lake of Fire. The interesting thing here is that in this passage we see *some* people who are at this judgment (more perhaps right before it), and are given rewards. These are millennial saints, not the wicked dead.

It's not talking about people today; if a man is lost today and winds up at this judgment, he will *not* make it through. He rejected Jesus Christ and the blood atonement for his soul. However, in the Millennium, there is no grace through faith in the blood atonement message of salvation. How could there be faith as we

82

know it today when Jesus Christ is ruling from a throne with a rod of iron in Jerusalem? By its scriptural definition (Heb. 11:1), faith is something you *can't see.* Everyone will know of and see the King of Kings. If there is an element of faith, it certainly is diminished from what it is today.

Jeremiah 31:34, "And they shall teach no more every man his neighbour, and every man his brother, saying, Know the LORD: for <u>they shall all know me</u>, from the least of them unto the greatest of them, saith the LORD: for I will forgive their iniquity, and I will remember their sin no more."

However the "salvation" is then, it won't be exactly like it is now. There will be a strict rule of law coming out of Jerusalem. If you notice, these servants and saints are looked upon favorably because they feared God – it doesn't say anything about faith. In the Millennium, people will be rewarded based upon their *obedience* to the commandments of Jesus Christ. A foreshadowing of His law can be found in Mt. 5-7.

VIII. Rightly Dividing within a Single Verse

We just looked at Rev. 11:18, and within it we saw over one thousand years into the future. This is a passage that was spoken by the twenty-four elders around the throne, within a vision of John, at the point in which Christ becomes king. These elders not only praise Christ for becoming king in verse seventeen, they prophesy in verse eighteen of what is going to happen one thousand years later! To top it off, verse nineteen is not spoken by the elders, and it goes right back to where the narrative left off with the events surrounding Christ becoming king.

What a book the Bible is! This book has so many layers to it! In one verse you can be reading about Christ's suffering, and in the very next verse you'll see Him reigning in the Millennium. At the end of Rev. 11, you see Him reigning at the beginning of the Millennium in verse seventeen, then in verse eighteen it is one thousand years in the future with the Great White Throne Judgment.

God wrote His book like this on purpose because He wants us to study it and rightly divide it. Jesus believed in rightly dividing the word:

Luke 4:17-21, "And there was delivered unto him the book of the prophet Esaias. And when he had opened the book, he found the place where it was written, The Spirit of the Lord is upon me, because he hath anointed me to preach the gospel to the poor; he hath sent me to heal the brokenhearted, to preach deliverance to the captives, and recovering of sight to the blind, to set at liberty them that are bruised, To preach the acceptable year of the Lord. And he closed the book, and he gave it again to the minister, and sat down. And the eyes of all them that were in the synagogue were fastened on him. And he began to say unto them, This day is this scripture fulfilled in your ears."

Jesus is reading this passage in the synagogue, and if you look at the passage in the Old Testament you'll notice where He stops reading:

Isaiah 61:1-2, "The Spirit of the Lord GOD is upon me; because the LORD hath anointed me to preach good tidings unto the meek; he hath sent me to bind up the brokenhearted, to proclaim liberty to the captives, and the opening of the prison to them that are bound; <u>To proclaim the acceptable year of the LORD,...</u>"

He stops right there! The reason He stops *there* is because that is all part of the First Advent. What comes next is His Second Advent:

"...and the day of vengeance of our God..."

That's the Second Advent.

"...to comfort all that mourn;"

There is the end of the verse, which applies to both the First *and* Second Advents!

What a book!

CHAPTER FIVE

ROUTE 666

"The highways lie waste, the
wayfaring man ceaseth: he hath
broken the covenant, he hath
despised the cities, he regardeth no
man."
Isaiah 33:8

THE THIRD ACCOUNT
Revelation 12-14

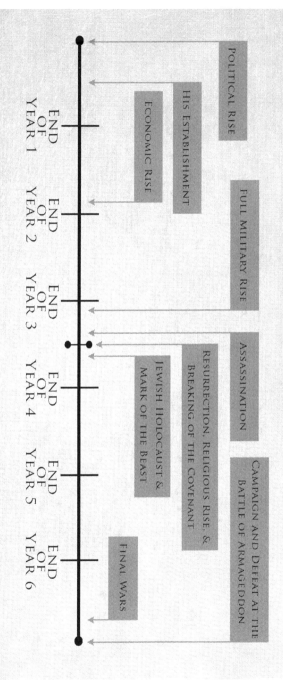

THE PATH OF THE ANTICHRIST AND HIS KINGDOM

POLITICAL RISE

HIS ESTABLISHMENT

ECONOMIC RISE

FULL MILITARY RISE

ASSASSINATION

RESURRECTION, RELIGIOUS RISE, & BREAKING OF THE COVENANT

JEWISH HOLOCAUST & MARK OF THE BEAST

CAMPAIGN AND DEFEAT AT THE BATTLE OF ARMAGEDDON

FINAL WARS

END OF YEAR 1

END OF YEAR 2

END OF YEAR 3

END OF YEAR 4

END OF YEAR 5

END OF YEAR 6

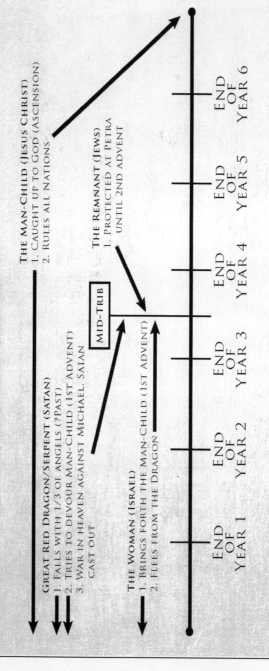

REVELATION 12

THE MAN-CHILD (JESUS CHRIST)
1. CAUGHT UP TO GOD (ASCENSION)
2. RULES ALL NATIONS

THE REMNANT (JEWS)
1. PROTECTED AT PETRA
   UNTIL 2ND ADVENT

GREAT RED DRAGON/SERPENT (SATAN)
1. FALLS WITH 1/3 OF ANGELS (?PAST)
2. TRIES TO DEVOUR MAN-CHILD (1ST ADVENT)
3. WAR IN HEAVEN AGAINST MICHAEL, SATAN
   CAST OUT

THE WOMAN (ISRAEL)
1. BRINGS FORTH THE MAN-CHILD (1ST ADVENT)
2. FLEES FROM THE DRAGON

MID-TRIB

END OF YEAR 1
END OF YEAR 2
END OF YEAR 3
END OF YEAR 4
END OF YEAR 5
END OF YEAR 6

ROUTE 666

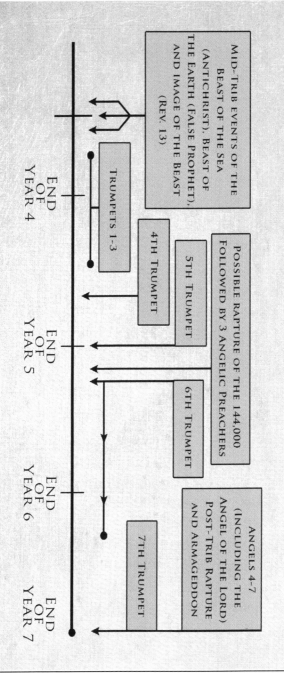

MID-TRIB EVENTS OF THE BEAST OF THE SEA (ANTICHRIST), BEAST OF THE EARTH (FALSE PROPHET), AND IMAGE OF THE BEAST (REV. 13)

TRUMPETS 1-3

4TH TRUMPET

5TH TRUMPET

POSSIBLE RAPTURE OF THE 144,000 FOLLOWED BY 3 ANGELIC PREACHERS

6TH TRUMPET

ANGELS 4-7 (INCLUDING THE ANGEL OF THE LORD) POST-TRIB RAPTURE AND ARMAGEDDON

7TH TRUMPET

END OF YEAR 4

END OF YEAR 5

END OF YEAR 6

END OF YEAR 7

I. Revelation 12

As we've already seen, the first account goes through the entire Tribulation, and the second focuses on the two witnesses and the Trumpet judgments in the last half of the Tribulation. The third account of Christ's Second Coming is very important because it helps the reader to understand the main characters that will be active throughout.

While the fourth account is the final summation of the story, the third account helps you to better appreciate the ending.

As far as a timeline, the story doesn't really start until chapter thirteen. Until then, we are just getting the background on the characters. In the first account, the parenthetical chapter was Revelation 7, the second account was Revelation 10, and the third account is Revelation 12.

There are seven personages described in this account:

1. **The Woman.** (Israel)
2. **The Great Red Dragon.** (Satan)
3. **The Man-Child.** (Christ)
4. **Michael the Archangel.**
5. **The Remnant.** (Surviving Jews)
6. **The Beast of the Sea.** (Antichrist/Satan's kingdom)
7. **The Beast of the Earth.** (False Prophet)

We start this parenthetical account in Revelation 12:1-2 where we see the first personage: **the Woman**. Containing striking similarities to Joseph's dream, she is clothed with the sun, the moon is under her feet, and she has twelve stars on her head. Without any doubt, this woman is Israel. She brings forth a **Man-Child** (Christ at the First Advent) who will later rule all nations with a rod of iron (Christ at the Second Advent). She then flees and hides from Satan in the wilderness for three and a half years. Christ doesn't come out of the church, and Mary isn't going to be fleeing the wrath of Satan anytime soon – the woman in this text is Israel. She is about to deliver when another individual enters the scene.

In comes the **Great Red Dragon**. Verse three describes this character: he has seven heads with seven crowns on them, and he has ten horns. Satan has always ruled over the Earth, in fact, he's called the *"god of this world"* in II Cor. 4:4. These seven heads and seven crowns represent the seven major kingdoms with which he's ruled the Earth. The ten horns represent the final summation of his power in the Tribulation – the ten federated nations* under the Antichrist. We'll go into this more thoroughly later in the chapter.

Verse four shows the origin of this monster, when he fell from the throne of God and brought a third of the stars with him. As we have seen before, the word "star" sometimes is used for an angel (Rev. 1:20; 9:1) in the Bible. We see the origin of Satan, and then the story picks up right where it left off again with the woman about to give birth.

[*The ten toes on Nebuchadnezzar's image are the ten horns and ten nations. Ten is also the number for the Gentiles. This could be ten literal nations, or the Earth may be divided up into ten separate zones of some kind.]

Satan stands by to destroy the Man-Child as soon as He is born. As already stated, this Man-Child will rule all nations with a rod of iron. It's a difficult stretch to see this as anyone but Jesus Christ. Satan trying to kill Him as soon as He is born represents the slaughter of the babies under Herod. Satan's plot fails and the Man-Child fulfills His mission. Lastly, He is caught up to Heaven, representing the ascension of Christ.

In verse six Israel flees from the Dragon for three and a half years. We are now in the middle of the Tribulation, when the Antichrist intensifies his persecution of Israel.

Satan has always wanted three things: to be worshipped, to have God blasphemed, and to annihilate the Jew. The story skips past the Church Age because it has little to do with Israel, and it also jumps past the first three and a half years of the Tribulation because, oddly enough, the *Antichrist is an ally protecting Israel during that time!* He has a covenant with them. In the Tribulation, the struggle between the woman and the Dragon begins when the Antichrist breaks the covenant and starts wiping out the Jews.

In verse seven we see a great battle between Satan and his angels and **Michael** and his angels. It's interesting to note that the angels are referred to as being Michael's angels, meaning they are under his leadership. This goes to demonstrate some kind of military hierarchy within the angelic realm.

How do angels and demons fight, and why do they do it? Throughout scripture we see in the spiritual realm there is constant armed conflict. Angels and demons (devils) battle each other in a very literal manner. Here we see the armies of Lucifer charge the very place of Heaven, and are turned back by Michael and his angels. What does scripture say about this sort of conflict that occurs in the invisible world?

In Daniel 10:11-13, 20 we see that one of Satan's strategies is to cause a *delaying action*. Someone prays for something to be done, God orders an angel to make it happen, and a demon does everything he can to delay its fulfillment. In this case Daniel prayed for three weeks while Gabriel was locked in combat and unable to reach him. What would have happened if Daniel had stopped praying? Do our prayers actually cause God to release some sort of spiritual power and strength to an angel that is acting our behalf? Many of these things we simply won't know until we reach the other side, but it's fascinating to consider.

In Daniel 8:9-11 the Bible tells us that the little horn (the Antichrist) will wax great and cast down some of the host of Heaven to the ground and stamp upon them. What is that? That is the war in Heaven and there is real damage being caused to the angels.

We know from Scripture that not only do angels and demons attempt to block and delay each other, they also amass in armies (II Kings 6:15-18).

Can an angel die? It's hard to tell. Angels are spirits (Heb. 1:7) so the question is: can spirits die? It would seem that they cannot according to what Jesus said (Luke 20:36), but that may just be in reference to the type of death we experience because the Bible also says that only God is immortal (I Tim. 6:16). Every man has a spirit in him, and while a lost man's soul may go to Heaven his spirit will return to God the Father (Ecc. 12:7). A human spirit is different than a soul and of the many things that it may be it is certainly the life source (James 2:26) given to a man from the Father, and when he dies it returns. Perhaps if an angel can "die," it will return, as any other spirit, back to the Father. Perhaps these angels will be spiritually resurrected at some sort of Judgment of the Angels in the future (I Cor. 6:3)? Once again, these are just interesting things to consider and they are not conclusively proven from the Scriptures.

Demons can be imprisoned (II Peter 2:4, Jude 6, I Peter 3:19-20), but there is no case of angels being held captive. It would seem that if warring spirits cannot die they can at least be contained and rendered incapacitated in one way or another

However angelic warfare actually occurs, it is for the same reasons earthly and carnal warfare takes place: *to hold or take territory*, be it physical or spiritual. Satan's hordes charge the gates of Heaven to try and take it, but the Devil loses this war and is now banished from the heavens. Before he was allowed to go right up to the throne of God (Job 1:6), but that day is over.

Being cast down to Earth, he now turns his wrath against the woman that brought forth the Man-Child. The Bible says she flees to the wilderness and is supernaturally protected by God in verse sixteen. She hides out for a time, times and half a time (three and a half years).

Satan goes to war now with the **Remnant**. "The Remnant" are the Jews that keep the commandments of God and have the testimony of Jesus Christ. Jesus told the nation of Israel that when they hear about the abomination of desolation standing in the Holy Place of the temple that they need to free civilization without so much as taking time to pack their clothes. This abomination of desolation is what we read about in chapter thirteen, a statue called "the Image of the Beast."

The Antichrist, as Satan incarnate, will at this point begin the worst holocaust of all time. Two-thirds of the Jews will be killed, and the last third will be refined by God (Zech. 13:8-9).

However, there will be supernatural protection for many of the Jewish people during this time. In Dan. 12:1 it speaks about the archangel Michael standing up for the children of Israel during the Tribulation.

We also see that when the Remnant flees to the place (This is probably the rock city of Petra within the land of Edom) in the wilderness that is prepared for her, then the Dragon casts a flood after the Remnant.

This could be anything: a literal flood of water or maybe an army of troops. Either way, the Earth supernaturally protects the woman. This flood is probably swallowed up by the Earth much like Korah and his people were swallowed in Num. 16:32. Do you remember Moses being involved in that incident?

Those in Petra are miraculously protected by God from harm for the entire last half of the Tribulation. They are fed with manna, their clothes don't wear out, and over a process of time they turn not only to God but to their Messiah, Jesus of Nazareth.

*Isaiah 42:11, "...let the **inhabitants of the rock sing**, let them shout from the top of the mountains."*

The Jews that don't make it to Petra will take the mark and worship the Antichrist, or they'll hide out anywhere and everywhere they can. Those that are caught will be tortured, killed, and put in concentration camps. The Jews that take the mark will probably be safe for awhile, but towards the end of the Tribulation (when the Antichrist is at war with seemingly everyone) the future Jewish holocaust will not be isolated to rebels.

II. Revelation 13 and the Mid-Trib Events

The camera panned over the crowd as a voice said, "It has been nearly three and a half years since the signing of the mutual protection act between Israel and the ten nations."

A second voice entered the conversation, "It's hard to believe all the things that have happened since then, but the most shocking and troubling of all is what we're looking at now."

A funeral procession slowly snaked down a pathway leading up the temple in Jerusalem.

"He loved Israel so much, standing by them continually and building this temple for them. It's so tender that he requested to be buried here."

"I just can't understand why anyone would want to..."

"Well, me neither. Even with all the good he did there are still dissenters. Word is that relations between the leader and three of the ten nations had been strained lately."

At that moment the procession stopped right in front of the temple, and the world prophet came to the microphone. The man was Jewish, and he was the greatest reason why Israel signed the covenant. He was a fiery preacher, promoting peace and unity in these troubling times. He often referred to the world leader as the "world's messiah."

"We meet here today to mourn and reverence the greatest leader this world has ever known. He fed and clothed the peoples of the world, and in a time when madness and hate wished to rule the day, he ushered in tranquility and stability. To those willing to follow the messiah, he has brought rest.

In honor of him, the people of Israel have constructed this statue that will be placed outside the temple that he built for them."

At this time a sheet was pulled off a ten foot tall image. It was a statue of the leader himself, with his hand outstretched.

"Behold Israel, your king!" the prophet said as he turned and faced the image. At this point, the next voice that was heard by the world was not the voice of a man.

"I am he that liveth, and was dead; and behold, I am alive for evermore!"

The statue spoke. It not only spoke, it had life. This was not some kind of Hollywood special effects stunt; this statue was really alive. The prophet had given it life. The statue turned to face the casket that held the body of the leader of the world.

Just then the prophet raised both his hands to the heavens, and fire began to fall from the sky. It didn't strike anyone, but it fell around the casket and lit it on fire. The crowd, half amazed and terrified, backed away from the scene.

The lid on the casket opened, and out stepped the Son of Perdition. He walked through the flames and faced the stunned audience.

"Fear not! It is I myself: for a spirit hath not flesh and bones, as ye see me have. I am your messiah, your king, and your god!"

The image spoke next. "Worship god and show your allegiance by receiving the mark he will give you. Any man who will not receive his mark must die."

With that strong delusion the Son of Perdition, False Prophet, and the Image of the Beast walked into the temple and right into the Holy of Holies. The

Antichrist sat down on the Mercy Seat and raised his fist towards Heaven...

In chapter thirteen we see the actions of the Antichrist, False Prophet, and the Image. They work in tandem to bring the world to worship Satan and receive the mark of the Beast. In verse five it says that the Beast was given power for forty-two months, showing that this happens at the three and half year mark. This ties in with the covenant being broken, the Fourth and Fifth Seals, the First through Third Trumpets, the appearance of the two witnesses, and Satan losing the war in Heaven. As you can see, the three and a half year mark is pretty busy!

There are three satanic beasts spoken of in Revelation. They are the Red Dragon in chapters twelve and seventeen, and the two other beasts in chapter thirteen (the Beast of the Sea and the Beast of the Earth). There is also a beast in Daniel that we'll look at.

III. The Great Red Dragon of Revelation 12 & 17

- The Dragon is Satan in Rev. 12:9.
- The Dragon has seven heads and crowns.

These heads are identified as being two things in Rev. 17:9-12. First they are shown to be the seven mountains where the whore of Rev. 17 sits. Secondly, the seven heads are seven kings. Revelation 17:10 puts it this way:

*Revelation 17:10, "And there are seven kings:
five are fallen, and one is, and the other is not yet
come; and when he cometh, he must continue a
short space."*

So you have five kings that have come and gone,
one that is here currently, and then one in the future.
These aren't five kings in the Tribulation that will
come and go, these are five kings in actual history as
we know it that have come and gone. The reason we
know this is because only one head is spoken of as
coming in the future.

Another reason we know these are kings in the
past is because the beast we are looking at is Satan*,
not the Antichrist. Satan has been the god of this
world for a long time; the Antichrist is only going to
run the world for a short period.

When we look at the beast that represents the
Antichrist, we'll see that the horns and heads on the
Beast of the Sea refer to kings and kingdoms existing
during the time of the Antichrist. The same applies
here also; the horns and heads on Satan refer to kings
and kingdoms existing *during* the time of Satan.

[*The main reason you know that the Beast the
woman sits on in Rev. 17 is the same Dragon of Rev. 12
is because they both are red. The other beasts are not
clearly identifiable as being red. At the same time
though, in the second half of the Tribulation, Satan is
dwelling inside of the Antichrist so in some regards the
passages concerning the Beast in Rev. 17 also apply to
the Antichrist.]

So who are the five kings that have come and gone? The best way to find that out is to start near the end and work your way back to the beginning. The seventh head is obvious: that is the Antichrist. The sixth head is spoken of as the one that "is." This refers to *the empire of Rome.* Rome was the great power of the world when Revelation was written, so that is to whom this is referring.

To find out heads five, four, and three you have to jump to the book of Daniel. In Daniel 2, Nebuchadnezzar has a dream about an image. The image is composed of different materials as it goes down from its head to its toes, and these represent different empires that were the superpowers of their time.

Nebuchadnezzar's Image:

Head of Gold	- Babylon (3)
Breast and Arms of Silver	- Media-Persia (4)
Belly and Thighs of Brass	- Greece (5)
Legs of Iron	- Rome (6)
Feet of Iron and Clay	- The Antichrist (7)

Heads five, four, and three are the kingdoms that come before Rome. The fifth is Greece under Alexander the Great, the fourth is Media-Persia under Darius and Cyrus. The third is Babylon under Nebuchadnezzar. As was already stated, the king to come who is only here a "short space" is the Antichrist.

Now that we've seen what heads three through seven are, that leaves us one and two to find out. While there are more than two superpowers before Babylon, there are only two that clearly dominated the children of Israel in their time. It would make sense that the first two heads would be the ones that affected Israel the most. They are Egypt and Assyria. Egypt dominated Israel for over four hundred years. While Assyria was not successful against Judah (the two southern tribes), they did carry the ten northern tribes captive back to Assyria.

But it doesn't end there!

Revelation 17:11, "And the beast that was, and is not, even <u>he is the eighth</u>, and is of the seven, and goeth into perdition."

There is an eighth head! At first this part is kind of confusing because originally it said that there were only seven heads. It becomes clearer when it says that the eighth head is actually one of the seven heads. It ***"is of the seven, and goeth into perdition."***

The Antichrist goes "into perdition" when he claims to be God and sits on the Mercy Seat in Jerusalem (II Thess. 2:3-4). At that point, he changes from the Man of Sin into the Son of Perdition. This occurs this after he has been killed and resurrected.

When the Antichrist decides to run the world from the Mercy Seat in Jerusalem, things go from *bad* to *worse*. The Antichrist is the seventh head and he is also the eighth head, but technically there are still only seven heads, because the seventh head dies and comes back to life again as a much worse monstrosity.

He and his reign in Jerusalem are so much *different* than the first three and a half years that it is spoken of as the eighth head, even though it is the seventh.

For clarity, here are the seven heads:

1. Egypt under Pharaoh.
2. Assyria under Sennacherib.
3. Babylon under Nebuchadnezzar.
4. Media-Persia under Darius and Cyrus.
5. Greece under Alexander.
6. Rome under the Caesars.
7. Rome under the Man of Sin.
7. Jerusalem under the Son of Perdition.
• The Dragon has ten horns.

These ten horns are clearly identified in *Revelation 17:12-14*, *"And the ten horns which thou sawest are ten kings, which have received no kingdom as yet; but <u>receive power as kings one hour with the beast</u>. These have one mind, and shall give their power and strength unto the beast. These shall make war with the Lamb, and the Lamb shall overcome them: for he is Lord of lords, and King of kings: and they that are with him are called, and chosen, and faithful."*

These are ten kings that will have power under Satan (the scarlet beast) during the Tribulation. It says they *"received no kingdom as yet"* – this refers to when Revelation was written. They didn't have power when Revelation was written – but they will have power under Satan during the Tribulation. The

103

Antichrist is not one of these horns; the horns are kings that work under him.

IV. Daniel's Fourth Beast of Daniel 7

To better understand the Beast of the Sea in Rev. 13, you have to take a look at the beast in Daniel 7. They're both the Antichrist's kingdom.

- **Daniel's beast has iron teeth in Dan. 7:7.**

This is very important to note because iron was the metal in Nebuchadnezzar's image (Dan. 2) that corresponded to Rome. It shows that the power of this beast is coming from *Rome*, where the Antichrist rules for the first half of the Tribulation.

- **Daniel's beast has ten horns in Dan. 7:7.**

As we saw with the Red Dragon, these ten horns are ten kings that have power during the Tribulation. In the first half of the Tribulation they run the show, but somewhere along the line there is a shake-up.

- **Three of the horns fall before an eleventh little horn.**

Daniel 7:20-21 "And of the ten horns that were in his head, and of the other which came up, and before whom three fell; even of that horn that had eyes, and a mouth that spake very great things, whose look was more stout than his fellows. I beheld, and the same horn made war with the saints, and prevailed against them;"

This other little horn is the Antichrist. While he is active during the first half of the Tribulation, he is much more powerful and terrifying in the second half. He is described as taking the kingdom by flatteries and words of peace during the first half, but once he has the kingdom firmly within his grasp it's completely different.

Somewhere along the line, three of the ten horns buck the Antichrist, and then they are defeated and subdued to his will. This is probably during the Second Seal, the Red Horse of war. The three horns falling before the little horn is what solidifies his kingdom in the first half of the Tribulation. Though there is war against him, he still comes through it maintaining the image of being a pacifist.

The following is clear about the ten horns:

1. There are ten in control when the little horn arises. Dan. 7:7-8

2. There are ten that destroy religious Babylon in the middle of the Tribulation, according to the will of the Beast. Rev. 17:16-17

3. There are ten horns at the very end of the Tribulation that have one mind and give their power to the Beast to go to war with Christ. Rev. 17:13-14

4. Somewhere along the line, three of these horns fall before the Beast and they are subdued to his will.

V. The Beast out of the Sea in Revelation 13:1-10

This beast is the Antichrist's kingdom, just like the fourth beast in Daniel 7. At the same time though, it also refers to the Antichrist himself. We know this because in the passage we see the world worshipping the Beast, and this can't be referring to his empire – it's talking about him.

This beast is like a leopard, a bear and a lion. We just got done looking at Daniel's *fourth* beast, but what we didn't look at were the three that preceded it. They are a lion, bear, and leopard.

The order of the three is interesting in both cases. While Daniel is looking into the future he sees a lion, then a bear and lastly a leopard. John in the future looks backwards and sees a leopard, then a bear and then a lion.

There are a few different ideas about what empires these beasts represent in Daniel, but the major point is that the Antichrist's kingdom will have the strengths that these kingdoms had. His kingdom looks like these three beasts because his kingdom is similar to them.

What these beasts are is a lengthy study in of itself; here are some of the different ideas about what these beasts represent:

Lion   - Babylon/Media-Persia/England
Bear   - Media-Persia/Greece/Russia
Leopard - Greece/Rome/America/United Nations

The Beast of the Sea, the Antichrist's kingdom, has seven heads and ten horns with ten crowns. The ten horns on him are the same as the ten horns on the Dragon; they are the ten kings that reign with the Antichrist.

The only difference is that the Dragon (Satan) has the crowns on his heads and the Beast (Antichrist) has them on his horns. The reason for that is because the horns are reigning at the time of the Antichrist, but they are not reigning during the entire time Satan is "god of this world."

Here are a few ideas of what the Beast's seven heads represent. The seven heads could represent the seven out of ten kings that stay loyal to the Antichrist in the first part of the Tribulation. Maybe he has seven heads because he looks like his master, the great Red Dragon.

It seems that the more plausible idea is the latter, because in Revelation 17 the Great Red Dragon has some things about it that make it look like the Beast of Rev. 13. They are two separate identities, but in a way they overlap because of the fact that the Dragon is *inside* of the Beast during the second half of the Tribulation.

VI. The Path of the Antichrist

While we are looking at the first beast of Rev. 13, this would be the best time to lay out all the steps the Antichrist goes through during his reign of terror on the Earth:

1. His rise in political power. While certainly some of it happens before the Rapture of the church, his major ascendancy on the world scene follows it.

The strongest indicators suggest that he is tied to Rome one way or another. Regardless, he'll use religion and politics to his own advantage to rapidly gain enough power to make some kind of covenant with Israel. He will continue to gain power by words of peace through already existing forums (such as the United Nations) and will begin to subdue nations unto himself. Rev. 6:1-2, Dan. 9:27; 11:21, 24, 32

2. His establishment. Just like kings of old usually had to lop off some heads when they first came to power, he will have to do the same. Three nations will rise against him in war, and will lose. He will come out smelling like a rose. Rev. 6:3-4, Dan. 7:7-8, 19-20, 23-24

3. His rise in economic power. Famine follows this war. The Antichrist, now in charge of the world's "peace and safety," will weaken the strong and strengthen the weak. Socialist policies will level the field and strengthen the Beast. Economies and currencies will change, the world's food and wealth will be spread out to everyone, and in the meanwhile he will levy a hefty tax. He will begin to control every facet of people's lives, paving the way for the mark to come later.

The Bible makes it clear that debt it is a trap and a snare, and many times a way to enslave people. Our nation's founders warned us about a central banking system in America, and twice the attempt to enslave

America to a central bank was shut down. The third attempt stuck, and we now know it as the Federal Reserve*: the bank that prints money for our treasury and sells us the paper. They charge us the interest on the paper they give us, and it would seem the only way we can pay off the interest is by printing more paper, and going deeper into debt. There is no limit to the amount of money drunk politicians can spend because they can always print more – and the Fed is always happy to charge us the interest.

[*For more information on the diabolical history of the Federal Reserve read *The Creature from Jekyll Island: A Second Look at the Federal Reserve* by G. Edward Griffin.]

That is only half of it: our government relies on other nations loaning it money to keep it afloat. The last president who got us out of debt, Andrew Jackson, also abolished the second attempt at a central bank in America. He knew that debt was a snare and it was the one sure way to control a man or a government. Now there is no going back. The financial system of our nation is now built on a system that God hates. God's way is freedom and personal responsibility; Satan's way is debt and enslavement.

The media will try and teach you that Communism is on the far left, Fascism is on the far right, and Socialism is somewhere in the middle. This is a lie. They are all big government, all designed to control you as much as possible. The truth is that there is big government on the far left and no government on the far right, also known as anarchy. The more government you have, the less freedom you have. No one is saying you can't have any government, but every time we add more we lose more.

Ironically, regardless of what "ism" it wears at the time, big government has never been guilty of what it has commonly been accused of: sharing and redistributing the wealth. Freedom lovers are interested in sharing the wealth as they see fit without the interference of the government. What big government wants to do (and will always do) is *consolidate and control* the wealth. The Antichrist's future financial grip of the world has its foundations in people *giving up their freedoms in the name of peace and safety.*

Our country was built as a constitutional republic, towards the right side of the bar with limited government. States acted independently with limited federal government interference and there was no central banking system. We are a far cry from that now. States rely on federal money for survival and bailouts, and the federal government relies on the Fed and other nations to keep it afloat. All the while our money becomes less and less reliable. The groundwork was laid *a long time ago* for our nation to be as the other nations.

Bloated government, debt, and the central banking system have put our nation on a crash course to be on the same socialist level as all the other nations of the world. Rev. 6:5-6, Dan. 11:20, 39, 43

4. His rise in military power. While certainly the initial worldwide war (Red Horse) is part of the

Antichrist's military rise, the Russian attack on Israel completely solidifies it. A Russian alliance attacks Israel while their guard is down, and God miraculously intervenes on their behalf. This alliance is decimated and gives the Antichrist the excuse he needs to invade these nations and further tighten his grip on the world. While always coming off as a peace-loving man, he is anything but that. Ez. 38-39

5. His assassination. Someone kills him right before the middle of the Tribulation. His lying, blackmail, backroom deals, and underhanded ways have finally caught up with him. Zech. 11:16-17, Rev. 13

6. His resurrection and rise in religious power. Satan now rules the world directly through the body of the Antichrist. All the world wonders after the Beast saying, *"Who is like unto the Beast and who is able to go to war with him?"* How can you beat someone you can't kill? The False Prophet proclaims him as God, and people believe it. The former one-world Babylon religion is destroyed, and in its place people are ordered to worship the Antichrist himself. Rev. 13, 17

7. His breaking of the covenant. At the exact mid-point of the Tribulation, the Antichrist enters the Holy of Holies in the rebuilt temple and defiles it. His image, a literal statue, is set up in the temple. This is the abomination of desolation standing in the Holy Place of which Daniel spoke. This statue is given life by the False Prophet and literally speaks. It is this statue that demands that everyone must take the mark and worship the Image of the Beast. Rev. 13, Dan. 9:27; 11:31; 12:11, Mt. 24:15-21

8. His Jewish holocaust and mark. Upon desecrating the temple, the Antichrist begins a war against all Jews that will not worship him, if not every Jew altogether. The Jews that make it to Petra are protected. A mark of loyalty is instituted, and people are commanded to take it and worship the Image and the Beast or die by beheading. No one can legally buy or sell anything without this mark. Rev. 13; 20:4

9. His struggle to retain power. Towards the end of the Tribulation, there will be more war. A king of the North, a king of the South, and possibly a third king, will war against the Antichrist, and the Antichrist will prevail over them. Many nations will be overthrown at this time. Dan. 11:40-45

10. His campaign at Armageddon. After these events, he will gather the ten kings and their armies at Armageddon to fight against God. He will attempt to wipe out, or at least imprison, all the Jews in Israel. A second army south of Petra will move to wipe out the protected Jews within the rock city.

At this point Zech. 14:2 says that *"...half of the city shall go forth into captivity, and the residue of the people shall not be cut off from the city."* We see in Rev. 11 that at the end of the Tribulation the two witnesses are beheaded in Jerusalem, and then three days later they come back to life again and ascend to Heaven. Immediately following this there is an earthquake, *in Jerusalem*, in which seven thousand people die.

It seems odd that in Zech. 14:2 that *half* the city is captured and that the *residue* is not *cut* off. It looks as though there is an interruption of some kind in the battle. The logical conclusion is that about the time half of the city is captured, Moses and Elijah are captured as well. The Antichrist announces this worldwide, beheads them, and makes a holiday out of it.

The campaign is stopped for three days, in mockery, to see if they will come alive again as they said. Three days later they do come back to life and ascend to Heaven, followed by the earthquake and the return of Christ. Rev. 11; 16:16; 17:12-14; 19:19, Zech. 14:1-2

11. His end. During the earthquake, the city of Babylon is destroyed. The army at Jerusalem suffers from divine maladies. The horses are stricken with blindness, and the riders with madness. The enemy soldiers' eyes, tongues, and flesh will begin to melt away while they stand on their feet.

Jesus Christ will appear in the sky south of Petra (which is south of Jerusalem), and wipe out the Antichrist's host from around Petra to Bozra, and all the way up north to Jerusalem. Once at Jerusalem, the heavenly hosts following Christ will participate in the battle with Jesus as the inhabitants of Jerusalem are rescued.

In the very end, the Beast and the False Prophet will be taken and thrown into the Lake of Fire. Zech. 12:4; 14:12, Is. 63:1-6, Joel 2:1-11, Rev. 16:18-19, 18:8, 19, 19:11-21

VII. The Beast from the Earth in Rev. 13:11-18

The last beast we'll be looking at is the Beast from the Earth. This is the False Prophet. He is the third member of the satanic trinity doing the work of magnifying and bringing glory to the Beast. He has supernatural powers along with the Antichrist, and gives life to the Image of the Beast so it can speak.

This beast coming out of the Earth can mean a few things. It could mean that he is of a single nationality, probably Jewish, as opposed to the Beast of the Sea (the waters in Revelation represent many peoples, nations, tongues – see Rev. 17:15) who could have come from a few nationalities. Coming out of the Earth could represent his being resurrected as well. Maybe he's someone from Israel's past, such as Balaam, miraculously raised from the dead for "these troubling times?"

What the two horns are for is not entirely clear. Horns on the Dragon and on the Beast represent nations. Being that the False Prophet is the religious leader of the Beast's empire, it could represent two religious nations brought under the sovereignty of the Antichrist. Perhaps they represent Vatican City and Israel; perhaps they represent Roman Catholicism and Islam.

He speaks as a dragon. No doubt he is a great orator, fiery preacher, and leader of men. He is given power by the Great Red Dragon himself.

VIII. The Mid-Trib Rapture of Revelation 14

Chapter fourteen starts out with the Rapture of the 144,000. These saints are the *"firstfruits"* unto God, in other words they are the first to get saved in the Tribulation.

In verse one we see them stand upon Mount Zion, and in verse three they are in Heaven before the throne of God. In between the two events there's a voice from Heaven that is the sound of many waters and thunder. These saints are raptured and brought to the marriage of the Lamb and his Bride, the church. They *are "redeemed from among men,"* and *"redeemed from the earth"* – they are raptured. *

As we've already seen, the church will be raptured before the Tribulation begins. Shortly after being raptured, Church Age saints will appear before the Judgment Seat of Christ to receive rewards for Christian service. After coming through this, the Bride is made white, without spot or wrinkle for the wedding.

[*Chapter fourteen is thought by many to be a parenthetical chapter, like chapters seven and ten are.]

However this event literally takes place, it will be an amazing and wonderful thing to behold. Unlike anything of this world there will be true, absolute, unblemished love between Jesus Christ and His Bride. The wedding, like most weddings, will be furnished with guests. Song of Solomon 6:8-9 describes many of these guests. They are people from other ages of time that *are not* part of Bride of Christ.

115

These guests are queens, concubines and virgins *without number* in SoS 6:8. When speaking of the Bride of Christ it says in verse nine, *"My dove, my undefiled is but one..."* In John 3:29, John the Baptist refers to himself as *"the friend of the Bridegroom."*

The queens and concubines refer to Old Testament saints. They are probably divided up before and after the law. The virgins without number refer to 144,000 and other Tribulation saints in Heaven (raptured or martyred) at this point. Remember the Tribulation saints in Heaven are referred to as a great multitude without number in Revelation 7.

We read in Matt. 25:1-13 about the ten virgins. They are brought in to *meet* the Bridegroom, not *marry* him. Do not confuse these with the Bride. The Bride is *one* chaste virgin, *one* body, *one* Bride* – what you read about in Matthew 25 is *five* wise and *five* foolish virgins. The five wise virgins are the Tribulation saints that are raptured up to Heaven to be there when the wedding takes place. The five foolish ones are ones that, for whatever reason, are not raptured. Over and over again, Christ's commandment to a Tribulation saint in Matthew 24, 25 and in Revelation is to be ready and waiting for Him when He comes. These that are raptured have met some sort of condition that will be made much clearer to believers during the Tribulation than it is now.

[*The Bride of Christ consists of people that are born-again in this age, placed within the body of Christ, referred to throughout the New Testament as being "in Christ." Being "in Christ" is the *huge*

116

distinction between people of this age and of other ages. The promises and commandments to the Jew in the Old Testament are not the same as the ones to those in Christ. One example is that we're told to love our enemies, pray for them and try to win them to Christ. The Jews usually prayed against their enemies and were often given the green light by God to wipe them out with *armed combat.*]

As for the timing of this event, it happens sometime after the middle of the Tribulation. Those who are marked of God are still here when the Fifth Trumpet sounds. The question then is who are the ones that have the seal of God in their foreheads? If it is only the 144,000, then that would put this rapture following the breaking of the covenant, then following the introduction of the mark and some of the supernatural plagues, and then happening sometime during or after the Fifth Trumpet. That is where it has been placed on the charts.

However, the other possibility is that every Christian in the Tribulation receives the seal of God in their foreheads. If that is the case it could change everything about when this rapture occurs. Scripture does not clearly state this however. The final thing to consider about this rapture is that there seems to be a conditional element to it (Heb. 9:28, Mark 13:32-37, Luke 21:34-36).

Following this rapture we see the actions of six angels and the Angel of the Lord.

IX. The Angels of Revelation 14

The **First Angel** we see in Rev. 14:1 is preaching the everlasting gospel. His message is to everyone on the Earth to fear God, give Him glory and worship Him.

The **Second Angel** comes out preaching about the destruction of Babylon. The city of Babylon is destroyed in the final moments of Armageddon. In Revelation 18, you see an angel preaching the same thing, and then saints who are living in Babylon are told to get out. The point is that when the angel preaches that Babylon is fallen (in Rev. 18) it actually hasn't happened yet – in a sense he is prophesying of what is imminent, it is a warning. The same thing is happening here. This angel is declaring to the world that the city that holds their economic security is as good as gone.

The **Third Angel** preaches to the world the warning of taking the mark. Everyone hears it, and everyone knows. The lines are clearly drawn; if you don't take the mark you can't buy, sell, or eat and you will be hunted down and killed. On the other hand, if you do take the mark you will spend eternity in Hell. If you aren't saved, trust Christ now so you'll never have to make that decision.

In Rev. 7 you see a multitude of saved Tribulation saints from every kindred, tribe, tongue and nation in Heaven. The only way that is physically possible in the Tribulation is for there to be literal angelic street preachers. There are over eight hundred separate languages in Papua New Guinea alone, and yet the

118

Bible says that people get saved from every language on Earth during the Tribulation. It would seem that for once in history – everyone hears the message!

What follows these angelic preachers is one who is *"like unto the Son of man"* reaping the Earth. He is asked to do this by the **Fourth Angel** in this chapter. The one on the cloud who reaps the Earth is Jesus Christ. Just like the fourth man in the fire with the three Hebrew children was *"like unto the Son of God,"* and Melchisedec was *"like unto the Son of God,"* this angel is the Angel of the Lord. If you count this One on the cloud as an angel, that puts you at (surprise, surprise) seven angels.

As we see the final events in this account take place we see the very end of the Tribulation as well.

The Earth being reaped is a final moment rapture of Tribulation saints, at the very end of the Tribulation. It's ironic that you have some who teach that the Rapture is pre-Trib, some say it is only mid-Trib and then others say it is post-Trib. The truth is there are three raptures within a seven year period! This last rapture is called the post-Trib, and obviously it is only for Tribulation saints.

This post-Trib Rapture is made very clear in Matt. 24:30-31, *"And then shall appear the sign of the Son of man in heaven: and then shall all the tribes of the earth mourn, and they shall see the Son of man coming in the clouds of heaven with power and great glory. And he shall send his angels with a great sound of a trumpet, and they shall gather*

119

together his elect from the four winds, from one end of heaven to the other."

The moment Christ appears in the sky, all who are believers will be raptured up to join in the army that is with Him. What an amazing moment! In the twinkling of an eye, those in Jerusalem who are fleeing for their lives from the soldiers of the Beast will be caught up to join their Messiah as he comes to Earth.

In Matthew 13 Christ tells the parable of the wheat and the tares that grow up together before the end of the world. The tares are gathered together to be burned (the nation's armies assembling together at Armageddon), and the wheat is gathered into the barn (post-Trib Rapture). In Matthew 13 and 24, and Revelation 14 the reaping is being done by angels.

The **Fifth Angel** shows up with a sharp sickle after this, and he is told by the **Sixth Angel** that the harvest is now ripe. The Fifth Angel thrusts in his sickle, and the next thing you know the blood of the Antichrist's armies comes up to the horse's bridle.

Two things happen at this moment. The most obvious one is the Battle of Armageddon; the other one is the instant world wide-death of all who have the mark.

Much preaching has been made of Luke 17 being the Rapture of the church, but the truth is the people who are *"taken"* are actually slain by the angels of God.

Matt. 13:49-50, "So shall it be at the end of the world: the angels shall come forth, and sever the wicked from among the just, And shall cast them into the furnace of fire: there shall be wailing and gnashing of teeth."

Christ's disciples asked about the two women grinding at the mill, and the two men in the field. They wanted to know what happened to the ones who were taken.

This was Christ's answer:

Luke 17:37, "And they answered and said unto him, Where, Lord? And he said unto them, <u>Wheresoever the body is, thither will the eagles be gathered</u> together."

There are three things that happen here:

1. All remaining saints are raptured.

2. All those with the mark are killed.

3. All those who do not have the mark but are not saints of God are left to enter the Judgment of the Nations.

As you read through Daniel, you see that though the Antichrist rules the world, there are always pockets of rebellion he is constantly putting down. There will be those that out of rebellion do not take the mark, though they never get saved. These are the people who will go on into the Judgment of the Nations. We will discuss the Judgment of the Nations more thoroughly in chapter seven.

Chapter Six

All Roads Lead to Rome

"And the woman which thou sawest is
that great city, which reigneth
over the kings of the earth.

And in her was found the blood of
prophets, and of saints, and of all that
were slain upon the earth."
Rev. 17:18; 18:24

Part One of the Fourth Account
Revelation 15-18

THE VIALS

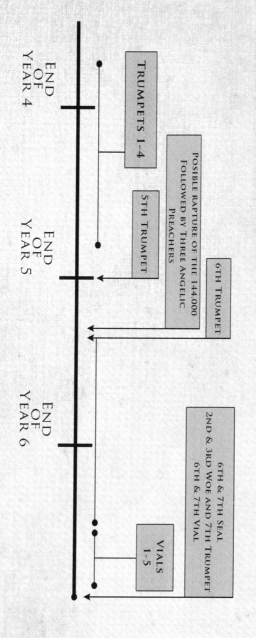

END OF YEAR 4

END OF YEAR 5

END OF YEAR 6

TRUMPETS 1-4

POSIBLE RAPTURE OF THE 144,000 FOLLOWED BY THREE ANGELIC PREACHERS

5TH TRUMPET

6TH TRUMPET

6TH & 7TH SEAL
2ND & 3RD WOE AND 7TH TRUMPET
6TH & 7TH VIAL

VIALS 1-5

Second Coming Events

6th Seal	2nd and 3rd Woe and 7th Trumpet	6th and 7th Vial	Matthew 24
Great Earthquake	Great Earthquake	Great Earthquake	
Sun Became Black			Sun Darkened
Moon became as blood			Moon Does not give Light
Stars Fall			Stars Fall
Mountains and Islands Moved		Islands fled away; Mountains not found	
Kings of the Earth	Kingdoms of this World	Kings of the Earth	Tribes of the Earth
	Voices	Voices	
Throne	Temple of God; Ark of his Testament	Throne; Temple of Heaven	Sign of the Son of Man in Heaven Appears
	Thunder and Lightning	Thunder and Lightning	Lightning out of the East
The wrath of the Lamb	Thy wrath is come	Fierceness of His Wrath	
	Great Hail	Great Hail	

I. Satan's System

Revelation 17 and 18 are parenthetical chapters dedicated to mystery Babylon, so before we go into the Vials we need to look at the subject that God set aside for two whole chapters of Revelation.

During the first half of the Tribulation, the world will be under a one-world religion. While there might still be some limited form of Christianity and other religions around at the time, they will start to be swallowed up by this one world religion that the Bible calls in *Rev. 17:5, "MYSTERY, BABYLON THE GREAT, THE MOTHER OF HARLOTS AND ABOMINATIONS OF THE EARTH."*

The False Prophet will lead this Babylon religion much in the same manner that John the Baptist prepared the way for Jesus Christ. In the first half of the Tribulation, the whole purpose of the Babylon religion is to pave the way for that moment of blasphemy when the Antichrist defiles the temple in Jerusalem and declares himself to be God.

Following that moment in the middle of the Tribulation the Antichrist, his Image, and the Devil himself will be worshipped by the world. As was stated before, Satan has always wanted three things: to be worshipped, to have God blasphemed, and to annihilate the Jew. Satan's system has always worked to accomplish those three things.

II. The Two Babylons in Revelation

We will see as we go along that there are two Babylons in Revelation. The religious Babylon is in chapter seventeen, and the political (or commercial) Babylon is in chapter eighteen. They both look alike because they are very similar. They overlap in their identities, because they *both* are the city of *Rome*. One is the religious side of Rome; the other is the political side.

You can tell you are looking at two separate Babylons in Revelation because of the way they are destroyed.

The End of Religious Babylon:

Rev. 17:15-16, "And he saith unto me, The waters which thou sawest, where the whore sitteth, are peoples, and multitudes, and nations, and tongues. And <u>the ten horns</u> which thou sawest upon the beast, <u>these shall hate the whore</u>, and shall make her desolate and naked, and shall eat her flesh, and burn her with fire."

First of all we see that this Babylon dominates the world when it is destroyed. It rules peoples, multitudes, tongues and *nations*. It rules over the nations, and yet it is the nations that destroy it. The only way this is possible is that it rules religiously.

The ten horns under the control of the Antichrist destroy this Babylon. This is in the middle of the

Tribulation when religious Babylon is dissolved so that Satan may be worshipped directly.

The End of Political/Commercial Babylon:

Rev. 18:8-11, "Therefore shall her plagues come in one day, death, and mourning, and famine; and she shall be utterly burned with fire: for <u>strong is the Lord God who judgeth her</u>. And the kings of the earth, who have committed fornication and lived deliciously with her, shall bewail her, and lament for her, when they shall see the smoke of her burning, Standing afar off for the fear of her torment, saying, Alas, alas, that great city Babylon, that mighty city! for in one hour is thy judgment come. And <u>the merchants of the earth shall weep and mourn</u> over her; for no man buyeth their merchandise any more:"

Here you see that it is God that is judging the city of Babylon and destroying it. Instead of the kings of the Earth being the ones destroying Babylon here they are mourning her. They are crying because of the loss of riches and merchandise; it has nothing to do with religion.

Rev. 16:16, 19, "And he gathered them together into a place called in the Hebrew tongue <u>Armageddon</u>. And the great city was divided into three parts, and the cities of the nations fell: and <u>great Babylon came in remembrance before God</u>, to give unto her the cup of the wine of the fierceness of his wrath."

We see in these verses that the destruction of political Babylon (the actual city of Rome) is at the end of the Tribulation, not in the middle as it is with religious Babylon.

III. Religious Babylon

Religious Babylon did not begin with Rome; in fact it began about 2,600 years before Christ with a man named Nimrod. The Bible says in Gen. 10:8-10 that Nimrod was a mighty man on the Earth and that he started a great kingdom. It says that the beginning of his kingdom was a place named Babel.

Nimrod's kingdom was contrary to God and in chapter eleven of Genesis God confounds the languages to break it up. Alexander Hislop's book, *The Two Babylons*, goes into great detail concerning the religion that came from Babel.

When Nimrod died, his wife Semiramis claimed that he was now the sun-god. Nimrod, extolled as the sun-god, was Baal. This is the same Baal that the Israelites had problems with throughout their history. It all started with his wife making him out to be a god after his death.

Not long after Nimrod's death his widow Semiramis gave birth to a son named Tammuz, or Bacchus. She claimed that the son was Nimrod reborn, as some kind of *messianic savior*. The sun and fire became the symbols for Nimrod (the sun-god), and the golden calf became the symbol for Tammuz, the child of Semiramis.

Yes, the golden calf problem that Israel had struggled with so many times started with this mixed up family. This family was so mixed up that Semiramis married her own son, Tammuz. Tammuz was worshipped down through the ages and is mentioned by name in Ezekiel 8:14. In a vision, Ezekiel sees women weeping for Tammuz inside of the LORD'S house, and God calls this an abomination.

The worship didn't stop with Tammuz though. His mother, Semiramis, got her fair share too. They were worshipped together as some kind of mother-son/husband-wife duo.

When God decided to break things up in Genesis 11 at the tower of Babel, this twisted religion managed to make its way into other cultures. The Chinese worshipped a mother goddess named Shingmoo; the Germans had the virgin Hertha; and the Scandinavians had Disa. In India she was Indrani; to the Greeks she was Aphrodite; and to the Romans she was Venus. Every time she shows up as a mother goddess accepting worship with her son/husband. In Egypt the mother is Isis and the child is Horus.

To the Israelites this mother-child idolatry was Ashtaroth and Baal. Over and over again they had problems with this religion. In Jeremiah 7 and 44 the Israelites had problems worshipping *"the Queen of Heaven."* This *"Queen of Heaven"* was Ashtaroth, a descendent of Semiramis. Baal was Nimrod, declared to be the sun-god by his wife Semiramis and reborn as the child Tammuz.

Later on in Acts 19, Paul ran into problems in Ephesus. Everyone was busy worshipping a mother goddess named Diana.

The hardest thing to do when it comes to winning souls is to get people to repent, whether that means admitting they are a sinner and need Christ or that they need to turn from their old religion. Now imagine what would happen if Christians began witnessing to people that had this mother-child idolatry ingrained into them for generations. Imagine if people tried to become Christians without repenting of this belief. Imagine if some people began mixing Christianity and Paganism. You don't have to imagine it; it already exists in the Roman Catholic Church.

Catholics are told to recite the rosary and pray to Mary. They bow to pictures and images of Mary all over the world. They are encouraged to pray to Mary rather than Jesus, because Mary is supposed to be more compassionate and loving than Jesus.

Do you realize that there was an idolatrous priest in the Bible 1,400 years before Christ that used images in worship (Judges 18:14)? This same priest went by the title "Father" (Judges 18:19), and took a vow of poverty (just enough to live by Judges 17:10). Certainly, all a coincidence.

Jesus commanded us not to give any man the religious title of "Father" (Mt. 23:9), and to beware of religious leaders who have an odd sense of fashion (Mt. 23:5). He also told us that he hates the deeds of those that put an overemphasis on religious hierarchy and titles (Mt. 23:7-8, Rev. 2:6).

130

Paul told us in the New Testament that we are not to confess our sins to anyone other than God and only through Jesus Christ (I Tim. 2:5). He also said that the day would come when seducing spirits of devils would try to command people to abstain from meats and forbid some to marry (I Tim. 4:3).

Catholicism is nothing more than a modern-day mutated form of Baal worship from 2300 B.C. Over the ages it has changed and conformed to absorb as many other people as possible. To absorb other people, all you have to do is add their beliefs to your own. This is what Rome has done since about 325 A.D. and that's how all roads lead to Rome.

The following are points from a compiled list by Tim Lahaye in his Revelation commentary, of Catholic heresies that have been introduced throughout the years:

- Prayers for the dead   300 A.D.
- Sign of the cross   300 A.D.
- Worship of saints and angels   375 A.D.
- Mass introduced   394 A.D.
- Worship of Mary   431 A.D.
- Priestly robes   500 A.D.
- Extreme Unction   526 A.D.
- Purgatory introduced   593 A.D.
- Latin worship services   600 A.D.
- Prayers to Mary   600 A.D.
- First official Pope, Boniface III   607 A.D.
- Kissing the Pope's foot   709 A.D.
- Worshipping of images and relics   786 A.D.
- Holy water   850 A.D.

- Canonization of dead saints   995 A.D.
- Fasting on Fridays and Lent   998 A.D.
- Celibacy of the priesthood   1079 A.D.
- Prayer beads   1090 A.D.
- The Inquisition   1184 A.D.
- Sale of indulgences   1190 A.D.
- Transubstantiation   1215 A.D.
- Adoration of the wafer   1220 A.D.
- Bible forbidden to laymen   1229 A.D.
- Communion forbidden to some   1414 A.D.
- Doctrine of Purgatory decreed   1439 A.D.
- Doctrine of seven sacraments   1439 A.D.
- The Ave Maria approved   1508 A.D.
- Jesuit order founded   1534 A.D.
- Tradition equal authority Bible   1545 A.D.
- Apocryphal books placed in Bible 1546 A.D.
- Immaculate Conception of Mary   1854 A.D.
- Syllabus of Errors   1864 A.D.
- Infallibility of Pope declared   1870 A.D.
- Assumption of the Virgin Mary   1950 A.D.
- Mary mother of Church   1965 A.D.

In verse four, this woman is decked in gold, purple and scarlet: the colors of Rome. In verse eighteen, she is a city on seven hills, as is Rome. In verse six, she is drunk with the blood of the saints of Jesus - no organization is responsible for the murder of more Christians than the Roman Catholic Church.

The religious Babylon you read about in Revelation 17 is the future of Baal worship. In the Old Testament, Baal worship was associated with fornication. As our age moves more and more in that direction, it is no surprise to see the future of the Baal religion include fornication in its worship (Rev. 17:2, 4).

IV. Political Babylon

Rome ruled the world when Christ came to Earth the first time, and she will rule the world when He comes the second time. When John saw the whore and wondered at her, it was because he saw a different Rome than what he was used to. John lived in a time when Rome persecuted anyone espousing Christ. Hundreds of years later under the Holy Roman Empire you had Christians being killed in the name of Christ.

Throughout history, the Vatican has influenced and controlled governments all over the world. If a king did not fall in line with the will of the Pope, an interdict could be placed on that kingdom. When this happened the sacrament would be denied from all Catholics within that country until the interdict was lifted.

Catholics see the Mass and sacraments as a means of grace so to miss it would mean damning yourself. The rites of marriage and burial would also be withheld. In the end, the Catholic populace would rebel against the king and he would be forced into doing whatever the Pope wanted him to, from killing certain people, to levying taxes to enrich the "Holy Mother Church," to turning a blind eye to the actions of bishops.

The *only way to be free* from the political power of the Vatican then is also the only way to do so now. It is to *win the hearts and minds* of people for the Jesus Christ of the Bible. When a country's people have their collective conscience ruled by a man in Rome, their government is ruled by that man in the same measure. A good Catholic is a citizen of two countries, the Roman Catholic institution and his home country. He is loyal to the laws and commandments of both, but when push comes to shove he must obey Rome.

During the Reformation, the political power of Rome was shaken as the consciences of people were enlightened by the word of God. The interdict did not hold the same power it did before because the populations of countries were not wholly given over to Catholicism.

In *The Secret History of the Jesuits,* by Edmond Paris, we see what the Roman Church did in response to the Protestant Reformation. A man by the name of Ignatius de Loyola created what is known as the Society of Jesus, or the *Jesuits*: men given the task of instituting universal power for the Catholic Church and thereby bringing in a complete universal Catholic Church by any means possible.

The Vatican had to change its tactics. It could no longer simply mass-murder people to obtain and maintain power. Now it had to try and gain power within countries internally through every facet of life. It was a Counter-Reformation designed to discredit and destroy Protestantism. This was done by infiltrating governments, schools, and churches. Rome traded the iron gauntlet in for a velvet glove.

When the Pilgrims came to the new world they did their best to stop the Jesuits from taking over America. Laws were passed to stop the infiltration of the Jesuits and the Mass was outlawed (J.T.C., *Smokescreens*, pg. 75). Measures were taken to prohibit any Catholic from holding public office in civil government. However, the time came when eventually the Jesuits were able to penetrate into the schools, courts, political offices, and military of the U.S.

Charles Chiniquy, in his book *Fifty Years in the 'Church' of Rome* quotes Abraham Lincoln:

"This war would never have been possible without the sinister influence of the Jesuits. We owe it to popery that we now see our land reddened with the blood of her noblest sons. Though there were great differences of opinion between the South and the North of the question of slavery, neither Jeff Davis nor anyone of the leading men of the Confederacy would have dared to attack the North, had they not relied on the promises of the Jesuits, that, under the mask of Democracy, the money and arms of the Roman Catholic, even the arms of France would be at their disposal if they would attack us. I pity the priests, the bishops and the monks of Rome in the United States, when the people realize that they are, in great part, responsible for the tears and the blood shed in this war. I conceal what I know, on that subject, from the knowledge of the nation; for if the people knew the whole truth, this war would turn into a religious war, and it would at once, take a tenfold more

savage and bloody character." (Chiniquy, Fifty Years in the 'Church' of Rome, pg. 296-297)

The goal of the Jesuits was to weaken the United States; this is why they supported the South. Divide and conquer was the goal. If the South had won the Civil War, they surmised that the Union would have been destroyed and the country would have been divided up into at least two sections. From there, our country could have been cut up and divided further.

According to Paris, the Jesuits played a key role in the First and Second World Wars. In a diplomatic document found in Austria-Hungary, Pope Pius X had expressed hostile intentions towards Serbia in 1913. The next year, Austria-Hungary had found a reason to go to war with Serbia.

The Vatican was behind Mussolini's coming to power in Italy. Both Mussolini and Hitler signed concordats with Rome which effectively made their nations part of the "government of God" and brought the blessing, support and stabilization from the Vatican. In fact, Vatican City was actually first established by Mussolini when the Lateran Treaty was ratified on June 7th, 1929.

Hitler said, *"I learned much from the order of the Jesuits."*(J.T.C., *Smokescreens*, pg. 20) If Hitler had won World War II, the world would have been plunged into a second Dark Ages of religious persecution against Christians. The Vatican would have ruled the religious world through the Third Reich.

Jack Chick in his book, *The Godfathers*, tells us that the Communist party in Russia was created by the

Vatican to destroy the disloyal Russian Orthodox Church. The Russian Czar was a protector of Russian Orthodoxy, so the Vatican had the government toppled. The Communists took up atheism instead of Roman Catholicism, so the Vatican sent in killing squads of their own called "the Ustachi" in an attempt to wipe out all the Russian Orthodox possible.

Rome doesn't get involved in politics? It's very likely if you dug deep enough you could find the whore involved in every major war since its inception.

Today, the Catholic Church does everything it can to try to appear Christian. Priests are seen at ecumenical movements, on Christian TV shows and often as special guests at megachurches. The Jesuits will take control of America one day. On of our jobs as Christians is to make sure that it's after the Rapture that they do so. *Catholic people are not the enemy*; they are simply lost sheep in the Devil's system, Babylon.

V. Where the Vials Start

Why do so many of the commentators call these things bowls? The text always calls them Vials. They don't call the Seals, stamps, or the Trumpets, flutes, but they always insist on calling these things bowls. A vial doesn't even look like a bowl! A bowl is something you put bean dip in; a vial is shaped like a Coke bottle. Try dipping your chips in a vial filled with bean dip and you'll see the difference.

So when do the Vials begin? Well, your first clue is in Rev. 15:1 where God says they are *"the seven last plagues."* So it's not during the first half of the Tribulation, and we can't really put it at the middle either because that's when most of the Trumpets are occurring.

A theory is that the Trumpets and the Vials are the same. The similarities between the two sets are remarkable, but they are distinct enough to see the difference. It would be tough to make the Vials the seven last plagues if they are the same as the Trumpets. We'll look at the similarities and distinctions when we view each Vial.

These Vials don't take place in the beginning or the middle, so it's sometime towards the end. These take place right after the Sixth Trumpet. If you remember, the Sixth Trumpet is the one with the 200 million man fire-breathing cavalry. They are on the Earth for a year, a month, a day and an hour. The lost that are alive after this horrific event are described as being very wickedly unrepentant.

The Vials follow the Sixth Trumpet because the Seventh Trumpet is the great earthquake, the two witnesses ascending and several other things that happen at the very end of the Tribulation.

In a previous chapter of this book we saw that there is a rapture that occurs before the Sixth Trumpet, so the 144,000 will be gone when these plagues occur, and there's a good chance that most of the Christians will be as well. It's interesting that Moses and Elijah will still be here, likely because their ministry will be focused towards the nation of Israel and God will want to give the Jew as much opportunity as possible to repent.

A quick recap: a rapture occurs about four months into the fifth year of the Tribulation, and following that, the Sixth Trumpet happens. The cavalry of two hundred million disappear after a year, month, day and hour. After that, you've got six months left in the Tribulation for the Vials to take place.

VI. Vials One through Five

The **First Vial** comes to pass with sores appearing on everyone that has the mark and worships the Image of the Beast.

It would seem that the majority of the populace of Earth has gone insane by this point. How could anyone keep their sanity after five months of mutant locusts that torture people, and over a year of running for your life from demonic cavalry? The description of mankind in Rev. 9:20-21 is wicked, stubborn, rebellious and insane. Law and order has gone out the window by now with over two-thirds of the world's population gone or dead.

To even try to picture such a time can make the carnal side of man doubt its veracity, but the Bible hasn't been wrong yet. If you are not saved, do not test the future of God's wrath. He loved you enough to send His Son to die for you, but He doesn't play games with people. Accept forgiveness through His Son's blood atonement while you can.

139

The **Second Vial** follows on the heels of the First Vial with all the oceans turning to blood. Everything in the sea dies. Ships are stranded alone in the middle of the ocean with dead crews. The filth and disease caused by such an event is unimaginable.

The Second Trumpet is similar to this Vial; however, there are a few differences. In the Trumpet, a third of the sea becomes blood instead of all of it, and a third of the sea life dies as well as a third of the ships destroyed. Also in the Trumpet you have the event caused by *"a great mountain burning with fire"* falling into the sea. In the Vial, everything dies and there's no explanation as to how it happens.

When the **Third Vial** occurs, people are shocked to turn on their faucets and see blood come out. All of the seas have become blood, and now all of the rivers do as well.

Unlike the Third Trumpet, this plague affects all of the rivers and fountains of water. The Trumpet has the waters being poisoned, but in this Vial the water becomes blood. With the Trumpet judgment, you have a star falling down and corrupting a third of the rivers; with this one, there is no explanation as to how all of the rivers and fountains turn to blood.

An angel pours out the **Fourth Vial** on the sun, and it becomes hot enough to scorch people alive. There is no repentance of sin at this time either; men keep on blaspheming God.

In the Fourth Trumpet, you have the a third of the sun, moon and stars being darkened. It is more similar to the Fifth Vial in which the kingdom of the

Antichrist becomes dark. This darkness is unusual; it inflicts pain. Men refuse to repent at this point, and we also see that they are still suffering the effects of the sores they acquired in the First Vial.

VII. Vials Six and Seven

When the **Sixth Vial** occurs, we are once again on the verge of Armageddon. In the Sixth Trumpet, there are four angels released from the river Euphrates, but in this Vial the river is completely dried up.

God *intentionally* makes it easier for Armageddon to take place by drying up this river. The Antichrist wants to rally all the troops together, and with the river dried up, the easterners arrive easier.

This brings up an interesting and scary side of God. If you are insistent on breaking your neck, God might just make it easier for you.

God is not sitting up in Heaven wringing His hands and worrying about the actions of rebellious and unrepentant people. In II Thess. 2:9, God is willing to facilitate people who won't repent by sending them *"strong delusion."* In II Kings 22, God wants *a "lying spirit"* to go and deceive King Ahab.

This doesn't mean God is a liar, but there comes a point where if a man wants a lie badly enough God will let the man receive a lie.

In the **Seventh Vial** we see the final events of the Second Coming beginning to take place. We are at the end! In the Seventh Vial we see much of the same thing as the Trumpets, ending with Christ becoming king.

Comparing the worldwide earthquake of the Seventh Trumpet with the one in the Seventh Vial, we have Jerusalem (the great city) being divided up into three parts, with a tenth of the city actually being completely destroyed. In this earthquake, seven thousand men die.

The declaration from Heaven is made, "It is done." This signifies that the Tribulation is over, just like in Matthew 24:29 when it says *"Immediately after the tribulation of those days..."*

The similarities between the Sixth Seal, Seventh Trumpet, Seventh Vial, and Matt. 24 are amazing. The chart on the following page demonstrates that it is just more proof that they are all the same event.

The globe shakes as the sky unfurls with thunder, lightning and hail. The sun and the moon darken as the only light that can be seen streams forth from the heavens...

CHAPTER SEVEN

THE KING'S HIGHWAY

"Behold, the days come, saith the LORD, that I will raise unto David a righteous Branch, and a King shall reign and prosper, and shall execute judgment and justice in the earth. In his days Judah shall be saved, and Israel shall dwell safely: and this is his name whereby he shall be called, THE LORD OUR RIGHTEOUSNESS."
Jer. 23:5-6

PART TWO OF THE FOURTH ACCOUNT
Revelation 19-22

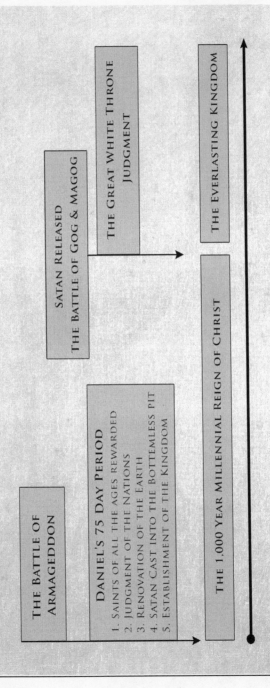

THE MILLENNIAL AND EVERLASTING KINGDOM

THE BATTLE OF ARMAGEDDON

DANIEL'S 75 DAY PERIOD
1. SAINTS OF ALL THE AGES REWARDED
2. JUDGMENT OF THE NATIONS
3. RENOVATION OF THE EARTH
4. SATAN CAST INTO THE BOTTOMLESS PIT
5. ESTABLISHMENT OF THE KINGDOM

SATAN RELEASED
THE BATTLE OF GOG & MAGOG

THE GREAT WHITE THRONE JUDGMENT

THE EVERLASTING KINGDOM

THE 1,000 YEAR MILLENNIAL REIGN OF CHRIST

I. The Morning of the Seventh Day

The Bible says in I Peter 3:8 that a thousand years is as a day to the Lord. The Millennium would then be the seventh day of human history, the Sabbath, a thousand years of peace, harmony and rest. Here is the conflict that led up to it:

B.C. 4004, Gen. 3:15:
After falling in the garden, the promise of a seed to bruise the serpent's head is given. Later the woman hopes this seed is her firstborn son, Cain.

B.C. 3270, Gen. 5:24; Jude 1:14:
The seventh man from Adam, Enoch, preaches about the Second Coming of Christ saying, *"Behold, the Lord cometh with ten thousands of his saints..."* Enoch is raptured; his son's name is Methuselah.

B.C. 2353, Gen. 6:
Satan attempts to fully corrupt the seed of man to prevent the fulfillment of the promise to the woman. The seed is preserved through Noah and God drowns the world.

B.C. 2126, Gen. 12:
The promised seed is preserved from Noah through Shem down to a man named Abram. Abram is given a direct promise by God that his seed would be a great nation, and that those that bless him shall be blessed and those that curse him shall be cursed.

B.C. 1911, Gen 17:
God changes Abram's name to Abraham. He is now promised that he will be the father of many nations. The promised seed goes to his son Isaac, not Ishmael.

B.C. 1760, Gen. 27:
Isaac's son, Jacob, steals the blessing from his brother Esau. Speculation is that the promised seed would have gone to Jacob God's way, but Jacob took things into his own hands. He then flees for his life from his brother's wrath. Later on, Jacob's name is changed to Israel.

B.C. 1689, Gen. 49:8-12:
On his deathbed, Israel declares that the promised seed, Shiloh, will go through his son Judah. A direct reference to the Second Coming is spoken as unto the promised seed *"...shall the gathering of the people be."*

B.C. 1635, Exodus 1-2:
The children of Israel, which had moved to Egypt, are now enslaved by the Egyptians. Satan moves to wipe them out but God raises up Moses to deliver them.

B.C. 1491, Exodus 15:
The nation of Israel is delivered from the Egyptians, and begins the journey that will eventually put them into the Promised Land.

B.C. 1451, Deut. 33:2:
Moses prophesies of the Messiah coming *"with ten thousands of saints."*

B.C. 1452, Numbers 22-25:
Satan again tries to corrupt the promised seed by using a backslidden prophet named Balaam. Balaam teaches Balak, king of the Moabites, to mix his people with the Israelites.

B.C. 1095, I Samuel 9:
Israel is now well established in the Promised Land, but rejects the theocratic rule of God administered by the judges – they want a king. God tells Samuel the prophet, *"...they have not rejected thee, but they have rejected me, that I should not reign over them."*

B.C. 1056, II Samuel 1-5:
Saul is killed and David becomes king. David is from Judah, from whom the promised seed is to come.

B.C. 1015, I Kings 2, Psalm 72:
In the declining days of David's life, the kingdom is passed to his son Solomon. David delivers a special Psalm to his son which describes the reign of the promised seed that is to come from their line.

B.C. 975, I Kings 13:
The children of Israel are split into two nations. The ten northern tribes go by the name Israel and the

two southern tribes (Judah and Benjamin) go by Judah. Solomon's son, Rehoboam, rules Judah, the tribe by which the promised seed is to come.

B.C. 742, Isaiah 7:14:

Isaiah prophesies to King Ahaz that the promised seed will be born of a virgin, and that His name will be Immanuel, which means God with us.

B.C. 609, Jeremiah 22:

King Jeconiah is cursed by God saying that "*...no man of his seed shall prosper, sitting upon the throne of David, and ruling any more in Judah.*" Therefore the future promised seed must be from a virgin woman of the tribe of Judah because all male seed from the line was *cursed* and could not rule *with the blessing of God.*

B.C. 4, Matthew 1-2:

The seed comes from a woman as was promised to Eve in the garden. The mother is from the line of Judah, as is the stepfather. Jesus is born and Satan immediately moves Herod to try and kill Him as an infant.

A.D. 23, Matthew 3:

John the Baptist introduces Jesus as the Lamb of God to take away the sins of Israel. Before Jesus Christ can be king, the Jews must repent and accept Him as the one to take away their sins. The religious leaders of Israel take offence at this.

A.D. 23, Matthew 4:

Jesus, the God-man, accomplishes what no other man in history had ever or ever will do: completely resist every area of temptation from Satan directly.

A.D. 27, Matthew 10:

Christ gives His disciples express orders not to witness to anyone other than a Jew. The objective is for Israel to repent, followed eventually by Christ reigning from Jerusalem. Following that, all nations would be drawn to the Messiah. In order for the Jews to believe, the disciples are given the apostolic gifts.

A.D. 27, Matthew 11:

It now is becoming more and more evident that the nation of Israel will not repent to accept Christ as Messiah. They want the millennial blessing without the repentance.

A.D. 29, Matthew 28:

The Messiah is given up by His own people and crucified. Jesus Christ, as the sacrificial Lamb, bears the sins of all time on Himself. Three days later He rises from the dead, proving Himself to be God.

A.D. 29, Acts 1:

No longer does the gospel go solely to the Jews. The apostles ask if this is the time that Christ will restore the kingdom back to Israel.

A.D. 29, Acts 7:

Once again the religious leaders of Israel reject the message to repent and this time they kill Stephen.

A.D. 63, Acts 13, 28, Romans 11:25:

The gospel has gone from being a Jewish-only message, to a mostly Jewish message, to a mostly Gentile message. The Jew has been put on the shelf and God begins dealing directly with the Gentiles. Instead of the Church Age only being a small blip on the radar, it's going to last over two thousand years.

A.D. 70:

Jerusalem is destroyed by Titus of Rome, and the Jews are dispersed.

A.D. 1948, Ez. 37:21-22:

Israel becomes a nation once again.

A.D. 20??, I Thess. 4, Rev. 7:

The dead and living members of the body of Christ are raptured up to Heaven. 144,000 Jewish evangelists are raised up to evangelize Israel and the world.

Half Way through the Tribulation, Rev.12:

The Antichrist tries to wipe out the Jews and the ones that survive flee to a place prepared for them in the wilderness. Moses and Elijah reappear to evangelize the lost sheep of the house of Israel.

Three Days before the Second Advent, Rev. 11:

The Antichrist's armies have captured half of the city of Jerusalem. A holiday is declared as Moses and Elijah are beheaded for the entire world to see.

Day of the Second Advent:

Those who see the sun, see it darken. The moon turns a dark bloody red.

The ground shakes as rain begins to fall in Jerusalem. The sky turns dark and cold. The severed heads of the witnesses suddenly attach to their bodies. The two men stand up and dust themselves off, then look up. The words, "Come up hither" are heard from the heavens as they ascend.

The shaking intensifies. Buildings tremble and fall. The soldiers in Jerusalem begin to panic and look for a place to hide.

A Mighty Angel is seen flying down from Heaven. He roars as a lion while he places one foot on the Earth and one foot on the sea. The Seven Thunders utter their voices, and with a hand raised to Heaven, the Angel declares this time to be finished.

Upon the declaration of the Angel, the entire Earth begins to shake violently. Great cities are destroyed and islands are cleared of all life by massive tsunamis. Men's hearts fail them for fear.

By this time, the city of Rome has been destroyed. In less than an hour it was destroyed with fire and brimstone falling from Heaven.

ROADMAP THROUGH REVELATION

While these events are taking place, the sign of the Son of Man appears in the sky over Jerusalem. Objects begin flying out of the air and hitting the ground.

In the city of Petra, the Remnant hear the tanks heading for them. From Jerusalem, the Antichrist has ordered his army south to move on the protected city.

To the north within Jerusalem, chaos reigns. The horses are stricken with blindness, and the riders begin to lose their minds. The soldiers' eyes, tongues and flesh begin to melt away while they stand on their feet.

The shaking stops. The heavens remain black. The giant Mighty Angel sounds the Seventh Trumpet.

Near the mountain that Moses went up to receive the law, voices are heard by the southern army of the Antichrist. The soldiers shake with fear; over and over again the voices proclaim, "The kingdoms of this world are become the kingdoms of our Lord, and of his Christ; and he shall reign for ever and ever."

The soldiers look in terror to the east. The black sky begins to fragment as multiple beams of light shine through. The voices grow louder.

The first thing that is seen is the head of a white horse.

One cannot describe the next sight that is seen on Earth and do it justice. The King of the Ages, He who is called Faithful and True, rides this white horse. Vengeance is in His heart; His eyes are as a flame of fire. In these eyes there is no compassion for those that hate Him on this day. There is only righteous justice, without a shred of mercy.

His Majesty, the Lord Jesus Christ, destroys the Antichrist's army near the wilderness of Paran. Heading up the King's Highway, Christ and the heavenly hosts pass the rock city of Petra to the joy of the believers inside. As they pass, going north to Bozra, a large group of angels split off from the host and gather all the remaining believers on the Earth within a twinkling of an eye. These believers join the host as they head towards Bozra.

The troops at Bozra are destroyed, and Christ's garments are dyed from the blood of the enemy. From Bozra, the host head straight to Jerusalem.

The heavenly army stops near the Mount of Olives. His Majesty steps off His horse, and when His foot touches the ground, it begins to vibrate. The ground splits open, creating a valley that heads towards the east and west.

Jesus Christ passes through the Golden Gate that has been sealed with concrete up to this point and walks into Jerusalem. As He looks to the sky it opens up above Him and the Ark of the Covenant descends to the Earth. The universe is silent as the God of the Ages sits upon it as King of King and Lord of Lords.

In chapter nineteen of Revelation we see the final mention of the Battle of Armageddon. The great whore is judged, the Antichrist's armies are destroyed, and the Beast and the False Prophet are cast into the Lake of Fire. The following are the twelve locations that Jesus crosses on his way to claim the throne:

1) The Wilderness. SoS. 3:6

2) Mt. Sinai - Deut. 33:2

3) Mt. Seir

4) Mt. Paran

5)Bozrah - Is. 63:1-6

6) Selah Petra - Hab. 3:3,12-13

7) Jericho - Zech. 14:3

8) Mt. of Olives - Zech. 14:3-5

9) Valley of Mediggo - Rev. 16:16

10) Through the Eastern Gate - Ez. 44:1-3

11) Jerusalem

12) Sits down upon the Ark - Rev. 11:19

Before the battle, in Rev. 19:7-10, we see the Marriage Supper of the Lamb. As we already know, this is an event for Jesus Christ and his Bride, the church. The marriage supper follows the Judgment Seat of Christ, in which the Bride is made spotless. While all these events are happening with the church up in Heaven, one must remember that the Earth is going through the Tribulation and the nation of Israel is being brought back to God the Father. Over and over again in Scripture we see the dividing line between Israel and the church. The church consists of New Testament saved believers, be it Jews or Gentiles, and they are wed to Christ. The nation of Israel consists of the biological race of people to whom pertain the promises given to Abraham.

II Peter 3:8 says that *"...one day is with the Lord as a thousand years, and a thousand years as one day."* As previously stated, in the whole span of human existence, we are now on day number seven -

154

the Sabbath. Hosea 6:1-2 says, *"Come, and let us return unto the LORD: for he hath torn, and he will heal us; he hath smitten, and he will bind us up. <u>After two days will he revive us</u>: in the third day he will raise us up, and we shall live in his sight."* In that verse it's clear that a group of people were set aside for two days (two thousand years) and then brought back to the forefront of God's attention on the third day! That group of people consist of the nation of Israel.

Following the battle and the marriage, Satan is cast into the Bottomless Pit in Revelation 20:1-3. After that the one thousand year reign of Christ starts. We see that in Rev. 20:4 Christ sets up the saints to rule with Him. During all this we find a unique time period of seventy-five days mentioned in Daniel.

II. Daniel's Seventy-Five Days

In the last few verses of Daniel 12, we are given two sets of days:

Dan. 12:11-13, "And from the time that the daily sacrifice shall be taken away, and the abomination that maketh desolate set up, there shall be a <u>thousand two hundred and ninety days</u>. Blessed is he that waiteth, and cometh to the <u>thousand three hundred and five and thirty days</u>. But go thou thy way till the end be: for thou shalt rest, and stand in thy lot at the end of the days."

As we've already seen, the abomination of desolation discussed here is the event that happens in

155

the middle of the Tribulation when the Antichrist defiles the temple and sets up his image. So the first time period that Daniel mentions here is 1,290 days *after* that event. The second time period that is mentioned is 1,335 days *after* the same event. What makes it really interesting is that there is a third time period after the middle of the Tribulation. That would be the standard forty-two months that are mentioned over and over again in Revelation, which would only equal 1,260 days.

To summarize, we have the standard forty-two months following the middle event of the Tribulation. This is 1,260 days. *Then* we have the extra thirty days (1,290) mentioned in Dan. 12:11. On top of that, we have an *additional* forty-five days (1,335) mentioned in Dan. 12:12! So what is going on with these extra days?

Here's what we know:

1) *The second half of the Tribulation only lasts forty-two months.* The Bible is very clear about that. There are verses in Matthew that hint that the Lord may "shorten" the days – but that means exactly what it says, He may shorten the days, but He's not going to reduce the number of them. Over and over again we are told forty-two months is the length of the *Great Tribulation*. This covers the 1,260 day mark.

2) *Matt. 24:29 tells us that the Second Advent will come* **"Immediately after the tribulation of those days..."** so what you can *know* from this is that the actual battle and some of the events right before it,

technically, are after the Tribulation. So the battle is going to fall within the thirty day slot. The battle isn't going to take one day, let alone thirty days, but it does fall into this time period.

3) Following the Second Coming, there is the Judgment of the Nations mentioned in Matt. 25:31-46. This is the first major event following the Battle of Armageddon. The Bible doesn't specifically state this, but it would make sense that the judgment occurs during this first thirty days, along with the possibility that the saints from all the ages being rewarded.

4) The next events in the timeline (the forty-five day period) would consist of the renovation of the Earth, Satan being cast into the Bottomless Pit, and the establishment of Jesus Christ's new kingdom.

These things previously mentioned are things that we know happen after the Battle of Armageddon, and they fall into the seventy-five days of transition from the end of the Tribulation to the beginning of the Millennium.

III. The Saints from All the Ages Rewarded

The whole point of the millennial reign is for God to honor His promise to a man named Abraham (Gen. 22, Heb. 11:39) and his lineage. It would be a little odd if the man to whom the promise of an earthly kingdom pertains wasn't there to enjoy it.

Matt. 8:11, "And I say unto you, That many shall come from the east and west, and shall sit down with Abraham, and Isaac, and Jacob, in the kingdom of heaven."

The Old Testament Jew still hasn't received the kingdom that was promised to him. In the above passage we see Abraham, Isaac, and Jacob enjoying the kingdom. Not only that, but Rev. 11:18 speaks of rewarding God's *"servants the prophets"* around the time of the Great White Throne Judgment. If they receive rewards, then there's the possibility that saints from other ages do as well. If this is the case, it will happen around the time of the Judgment of the Nations.

IV. The Judgment of the Nations

The primary text for this judgment is Matthew 25:31-46. This chapter provides one of the biggest reasons why it is important to rightly divide the word of truth as we're commanded to in II Timothy 2:15.

If you study your New Testament you know *you* are *saved* by grace, *kept* by grace, and that there's nothing *you* can do about it either way once you are saved. Studying the Bible means understanding that *there are no contradictions in it!* When two passages contradict – they're both right. We may not understand how that can be, but the word of God is perfect and that means believing it, even when our very weak and finite minds don't understand it.

What the Catholic never thought of (when he said that this passage was proof that we all needed to work our way to Heaven) was that maybe the people being judged here aren't Christians. The people that are at this judgment have to have gone through several filters to make it to this point.

1) They can't be saved Christians. They were all raptured at the very beginning of this whole thing.

2) They can't be people who have the mark on them; they all were wiped out at the time of the Second Coming.

3) They can't be Tribulation saints, because they were raptured out at the middle and end of the Tribulation.

4) They can't be the Jewish Remnant. At this point the surviving nation of Israel is completely converted over to Christ, and raptured.

That only leaves one category. The people at this judgment are unsaved people who never took the mark. They did not accept Christ during the Tribulation but at the same time, for whatever reason, they did not sign on with the Antichrist and take his mark.

All the nations of remaining unsaved people stand before Christ at this judgment. From here, individuals are separated from these nations and designated as sheep or goats. They are then judged as sheep or goats. Those judged as sheep go into life eternal, and those judged to be goats go into everlasting punishment (Matt. 25:46). Nowhere in Scripture is any individual thrown in Hell because he belonged to a nation, and there's no reason to think that is what this is about. The nations are divided, and the sheep and the goats are people, not entire nations.

Nobody has a problem with faith or submission to God at this point, everyone believes Jesus is who He is, and that He did what He did. These people are judged based upon one thing only: how they treated Christ's brethren, the Jews. This is one of the greatest fulfillments of the promise given to Abraham, *"And **I will bless them that bless thee, and curse him that curseth thee**: and in thee shall all families of the earth be blessed." Genesis 12:3*

This is a stark reminder that the Tribulation period is *all about Israel* and her Messiah. It has nothing to do with the church as we know it to be today.

Those that survive this judgment are forgiven of their sins and given eternal life. They are made clean, and are allowed to enter Christ's kingdom to live forever. We understand this based upon *Matt. 25:46, "And these shall go away into everlasting punishment: but the righteous into life eternal."*

From there we have to make some rational conclusions. These individuals have children, who do not have the same guarantee of eternal life that they did. How do we know that? Because right now on the timeline we are at the end of the Tribulation, heading into the Millennium; and someone has kids.

These kids have more kids, and more kids, and more kids, until eventually most of them turn bad and go against Christ at the end. The people that are reproducing are the same people that made it through this judgment and were granted eternal life. They are like Adam and Eve, and are given the task of populating the Earth to the glory of God. They still

160

have the old nature in them, because their children have the old nature.

So that may leave us wondering what we'll be like at this point and what the Tribulation saints or even the Old Testament saints will be like. We know that we'll be like Christ and have a gloried body.

I John 3:2, "Beloved, now are we the sons of God, and <u>*it doth not yet appear what we shall be*</u>*: but we know that, when he shall appear, we shall be like him; for we shall see him as he is."*

As for the Old Testament saints, we know one thing – they do have resurrected bodies. Job said, *"And though after my skin worms destroy this body,* <u>*yet in my flesh shall I see God:"*</u> *(Job 19:26)* Job said *in his flesh* he would see God. He's talking about something other than the dust in his coffin right now.

It is reasonable to assume the same case with the Tribulation saints. They either die or are raptured at the end, just like us (only we're raptured at the beginning). They are going to have resurrection bodies too. The only difference in these groups is that the Church Age saints are designated as being part of the body of Christ. So, our resurrection bodies may be different than theirs, but just like John said, *"...it doth not yet appear..."* If John said it isn't exactly clear what we're going to be, let's leave it at that!

V. The Renovation of the Earth

First of all, you have to remember that the Earth has gone through the seven-year Tribulation filled with

161

wars, disease, famine – curse after curse after curse including one-third of the trees being burnt, the streams and rivers being poisoned, and everything and everyone in the sea being killed.

God doesn't leave it that way; he fixes it before the Millennium starts. In fact, In Amos 9:13 during the Millennium the Bible says that the *"...the plowman shall overtake the reaper,"* meaning the Earth will be blessed to the point that there will be an overabundance of food for the whole world. There will be no such thing as food drives, or charities for the hungry, or foreign aid from America to help starving people in Asia and Africa.

The physical landscape of the Earth is restored to something wonderful, something better than it is now (Is. 11:1-10, Amos 9:13, Hos. 2:18, Is. 35:1-10, Is. 65:20-25).

VI. The New Covenant is Accepted.

The New Covenant was offered to the Jews at the First Advent, but it was rejected time and time again. Think of it like this: the nation of Israel had a choice: operate under the old contract or accept the terms of the new contract. They had already signed onto the old contract under Moses, but the old contract had an expiration date. *Hebrews 8:13* says, *"In that he saith, A new covenant, he hath made the first old. Now that which decayeth and waxeth old is ready to vanish away."* Israel stood there, looking at the expiration date on the old contract and the terms of the new contract, and chose to not sign.

Right now Israel is still under the old contract, a contract that has completely faded away and is worthless. During the Tribulation they will agree to the terms of the new contract: recognize and accept Jesus Christ as their Saviour, Redeemer and King. They will then reap the benefits: national forgiveness and salvation, complete fulfillment of the Abramic Covenant, safety forever, and the resurrection of their saints (Is. 59:20-21, Ez. 11:19-20, Jer. 31:31-34, Jer. 23:5-8; 33:15-16, Hos 3:5, Ez. 36:24-28, Matt. 8:11)

VII. Hell, Bottomless Pit, and the Lake of Fire

Rev. 20:1-3, "And I saw an angel come down from heaven, having the key of the bottomless pit and a great chain in his hand. And he laid hold on the dragon, that old serpent, which is the Devil, and <u>Satan, and bound him a thousand years, And cast him into the bottomless pit</u>, and shut him up, and set a seal upon him, that he should deceive the nations no more, till the thousand years should be fulfilled: and after that he must be loosed a little season."

Now it looks as though before the final touches are made on setting up positions of authority on Earth, Satan is cast into the Bottomless Pit. That may seem odd at first, when you think about it. Really, let's think about the timeline here. First, we have the Beast and the False Prophet thrown into the Lake of Fire, then we have the Judgment of the Nations, then we have the renovation of the Earth, and then right before the Bible speaks of the one thousand year reign beginning in Rev. 20:4 – we have Satan cast into the Bottomless Pit. It's almost like the Lord made him (the Devil) stick around and see what He was going to do to the Earth with Satan gone. It appears as though God will be "one-upping" Satan. Would He do that? Read the book of Job.

So after at least six thousand years of causing havoc on Earth, Satan is cast into the Bottomless Pit. He is to reside there for one thousand years. There are a lot of ideas about what the Bottomless Pit is, but the only thing we can know for sure is that it doesn't have a bottom. It would make sense that it is some sort of place where the gravitational pull would make one feel like he was continually falling. It's likely that it's in the center of the Earth and as the Earth spins the individual keeps falling.

The Lake of Fire and Hell are not one and the same. In Luke 16, we see the story of the rich man and Lazarus. The rich man is in Hell which at that time was across from Paradise, also called Abraham's Bosom. Both were in the center of the Earth. All of Paradise was moved up to the third heaven where Christ dwells (I Cor. 12:1-5). This took place when Christ *"led captivity captive"* in Eph. 4:8. While Christ's body was in the tomb, His soul was in the heart of the Earth (Matt. 12:40) for three days, and after three days He brought the souls in Paradise up to the third heaven with Him. Is. 5:14 says that *"hell hath enlarged herself,"* meaning that the space that was left vacant by Paradise was filled by Hell.

The Lake of Fire is different than what Hell is today. You can call the Lake of Fire "Hell" because technically Hell goes into the Lake of Fire (Christ calls it Hell in Matt. 9). But in the interest of distinguishing the two places, the Lake of Fire doesn't actually exist yet. The Lake of Fire goes through two periods.

First, it is created during the process of Armageddon; we know that because there is no indication that it exists until the Beast and the False Prophet are cast into it. Once they are in it they do not burn up into nothing; they are there the entire one thousand years that Satan is in the Bottomless Pit. We know this because after Satan spends one thousand years in the Bottomless Pit he winds up going from there to the Lake of Fire – and the Beast and the False Prophet are both still there (Rev. 20:10).

But before that happens, the lost are still in Hell during the Millennium. The Lake of Fire's location is on the Earth during the Everlasting Kingdom (This is the kingdom of Christ that follows the Millennium and goes out into eternity. Is. 66:24), so perhaps it is also on Earth during the millennial reign. If that is the case, then perhaps instead of people going to Hell in the Millennium they go to the Lake of Fire on Earth.

The second stage of the Lake of Fire is after the Millennium. In Rev. 20:11-15, Hell delivers up the people in it, they are then judged at the Great White Throne Judgment, and then they go into the Lake of Fire.

Is. 66:24, "And they shall go forth, and look upon the carcases of the men that have

165

transgressed against me: for <u>their worm</u> shall not die, neither shall their fire be quenched; and they shall be an abhorring unto all flesh."

In this verse, people are seeing others suffering in fire while on Earth. The passage is after the Battle of Armageddon and after the new heavens and new Earth is created. We know that because of the condition of the people here, a condition that is not achieved until after the Great White Throne Judgment.

The next thing we're going to look at in regards to the Lake of Fire is important, and to ignore it is to ignore something that Christ thought was important. Christ said three times in one sermon these words:

"Where their worm dieth not, and the fire is not quenched."

You'll find that sermon in Mark 9. Jesus is quoting Is. 66:24 – *a verse He quotes more than any other* in the New Testament. We see in that verse a series of words that lead to a very shocking conclusion, the words are *"carcases of the men"* and *"their worm."* The words *"their worm"* is in the possessive case and it reflects back *to "the carcases of men."*

Right now, if you are saved, if you were to die, your soul would go to Heaven. Your body would go in the ground. At the resurrection, your body and soul will be reunited. Your body will be changed to a glorious new body, a different body.

Right now, if you are lost, if you were to die, your soul would go to Hell. Your body would go to the ground. There will be a time when your body and your soul will be reunited. There will be a resurrection of the dead for the lost man. The lost man will get a different body before he goes into the Lake of Fire. If we get a body like our Saviour, it is a conceivable explanation that what Jesus was speaking about was the lost getting a body like their father the Devil, a body like a serpent or a worm.

VIII. The Millennial Reign of Christ

There are a lot of events in chapter twenty of Revelation, if you haven't noticed! We've had to jump around a lot to explain the events that happen during the first seventy-five days. As we saw, it is impossible to talk about the Bottomless Pit and the Lake of Fire without jumping forward and looking at the Great White Throne Judgment, which is one thousand years after Satan is initially thrown into the Bottomless Pit. If it's confusing, please consult the charts.

In Rev. 20:4-6, we see the saints of the Tribulation taking part in the *First Resurrection* at the beginning of the Millennium. These saints are given authority to rule and reign with Christ for one thousand years. We also see a reference to the *Second Resurrection*, which we already discussed when we looked at the Lake of Fire.

There are two resurrections. The first one is broken up into two separate parts. I Cor. 15:22-24 best describes the two parts of the First Resurrection.

I Cor. 15:22-24, "For as in Adam all die, even so in Christ shall all be made alive. But every man in his own order: Christ the firstfruits; afterward they that are Christ's at his coming. Then cometh the end, when he shall have delivered up the kingdom to God, even the Father; when he shall have put down all rule and all authority and power."

"Christ the firstfruits" would be Christ and those that bodily arose with Him at the resurrection.

"They that are Christ's at his coming" would be the raptures/resurrections throughout the events of the Second Coming.

"Then cometh the end" does not refer to a resurrection of the just; it refers to events in the Everlasting Kingdom.

Following the resurrection of just, the Millennium begins. Christ rules and reigns on Earth for one thousand years. During this time, there is peace on Earth and good will towards men. There has never been peace on Earth, good will towards men and there never will be until Jesus Christ makes it happen.

Christ will reign (Ps. 72:7-11; 32:1-2) with a rod of iron, meaning His word is law. Reigning with Him will be Church Age Christians (II Tim. 2:12), the twelve Jewish apostles (Matt. 19:28), and martyred Tribulation saints (Rev. 20:4).

The law will be established (Is. 2:1-4) on the Earth once again, the temple rebuilt (Ez:40-44) and Christ will reign from Jerusalem, the city of the great King (Ps. 9:11, Is. 60:14). All the nations (Is. 60:1-3, 10-12, Zech. 8:20-23; 13:1-3,6) will come up annually to worship the King (Zech 14:16-19). Kids will have snakes, lions, wolves and bears for pets. There will be no such thing as natural predators (Is. 11:6-10).

The serpent will still be on his belly "eating dust" (Is. 65:25) as he was cursed to in Gen 3. The curse is lifted off the Earth, but apparently not off the serpent.

Contrary to what is taught by many, the healing element in the atonement does not come to fruition until the Millennium. Those who relegate Christians who die of a sickness to the ranks of the faithless and unbelieving are wrong. They fail to teach the fact that some promises in the Bible do not apply to us, that most prophecies about Christ are yet to be fulfilled and that Israel is *not* the church.

Yes, there are those that need to learn, or are confused and searching, but there is no excuse for a leader of a church to try and lay false guilt on someone because he's sick and going to die. Bad things happen to good people because we're on a sin-cursed Earth. While the Earth is still cursed we'll still get sick and die.

But people do not get sick in the Millennium. Isn't that amazing? No such thing as cancer, emphysema, a cold, the flu, multiple sclerosis and Alzheimer's (Is. 33:24, Ps. 103:3)! In some way, the curse is lifted off the Earth and a lot of bad things are gone with it. It wouldn't be surprising to find that there are no such things as miscarriages or any form of birth complications.

During this time, there will be no temptation from Satan because he will be locked up. There will also be no temptation from the world's system. Jesus Christ will make sure that there is no such thing as *"worldly temptation"* when He is ruling the world. The only temptation that will exist will come from the sinful, deprived nature of man. Man will no longer be able to complain about a bad upbringing, his environment, his circumstances, or blame things on the Devil making him do it.

The heart of man is never satisfied, and after the one thousand years are complete, Satan will be released to go out and deceive the nations. They will gather together against Jerusalem to try and destroy the King of Kings. The Bible says the number that comes against the *"camp of the saints"* will be as the sand of the sea. There will be far more in Satan's army this time than there was at the Battle of Armageddon; this is the battle of Gog and Magog. It's not really much of a fight though. Before anyone knows what's going on fire will come out of Heaven and consume them. Then Satan is cast into the Lake of Fire. This marks the end of the Millennium.

IX. The Great White Throne Judgment

What we see here is the last and final judgment in the Bible, and it is the most terrifying. Here the lost man finally gets the opportunity to be judged according to his works.

Before that happens though, the Bible says that the Heaven and Earth *"fled away"* from the face of Him that sat on the Great White Throne. This is a reference to the universe being dissolved before this judgment.

II Peter 3:12, "Looking for and hasting unto the coming of the day of God, wherein the <u>heavens</u>

__being on fire shall be dissolved,__ and the elements shall melt with fervent heat?"

This universe will be destroyed, down to the very elements. At that point, the dead in their sins will stand before God to be judged according to their works.*

Every lost soul will stand before God to give account. The secrets of the heart will be made manifest and everyone will stand guilty before God. The lost man will be judged according to his works, and those not found in the book of life will be cast into the Lake of Fire. This is the second death.

[*Around this time saints from the Millennium will receive rewards (Rev. 11:18). The most logical explanation is that they receive them before this judgment, as all indicators are that it's only the wicked dead judged here]

X. The Everlasting Kingdom and the New Heavens and New Earth

Even with Christ at the helm, the Millennial Kingdom will not be perfect. The reason for this, of course, has nothing to do with Jesus Christ – it's because the people in the kingdom won't be perfect! But all that changes after the Great White Throne Judgment.

After the judgment was finished, all eyes looked towards the Great White Throne. Any tears that remained had been wiped away. The saints now understood there was no more sin, and consequently no

171

more death. They looked in anticipation as to what would happen next.

A voice, as the sound of many waters, came forth from the throne saying, "Behold, I make all things new."

Within a moment, the Earth and everything therein began to disintegrate until there was nothing left. The planets, stars, solar systems - all began to burn with a fervent heat.

And for an indeterminable amount of time, the hosts of Heaven watched as The Great I Am spun a new Earth and new heavens into existence. The morning stars sang together and the sons of God shouted for joy as the Lord created a new and perfect universe.

At some point, the holy city, New Jerusalem descended towards the Earth. While living on Earth the Christians had called this city "Heaven," and now it looked like there was going to be Heaven on Earth. This city was twelve hundred miles tall, wide, and high. The city was of pure gold, so pure that it was transparent. The foundations of the city were not completely clear; they were made of many precious stones. There were green emeralds, blue sapphires, yellow and orange topazes, purple, brown, and red stones all so beautiful and pure. There were twelve foundations, and arranged within these twelve foundations were the names of the twelve Jewish apostles.

This city had twelve gates, and the gates were giant pearls. Each gate was one solid pearl. Written on these pearls were the names of the twelve tribes of Israel. As Rome was called Satan's bride, this city is the Lamb's

Bride. It is the eternal home for those saved during the Church Age, the members of the Body of Christ.

The city was pure. Clean. There was no such thing as litter, pollution, profanity, or indecency. You couldn't smell alcohol, cigarette smoke, car fumes, marijuana, or any of the other filth and stench of the cities that were held in such high regard on the prior Earth.

Within the city, there was no such thing as night, and there was no need for the sun. The Lamb was the light thereof.

There was the throne of God and of the Lamb, and coming out at the foot of it was a clear river. An enormous tree grew through the middle of this stream and its roots spread out to both shores of the river. It grew twelve different types of fruit. This tree was the same tree that Adam saw, the tree of life.

Following the Millennial Kingdom, and then the Great White Throne Judgment, the next period of time is the Everlasting Kingdom of Jesus Christ (II Peter 1:11). People in this kingdom are all sinless, perfect human beings. The reason we know this is because there is no more death (I Cor. 15:26). The wages of sin is death, so if there is no more death then there is no more sin.

Now what do you think would happen if there was no death? What do you think would happen if there was nothing but sinless human beings on Earth, living, breathing, and multiplying?

Have you ever wondered what would have happened if Adam and Eve never sinned, and kept having children? Consider another question: do you think God rigged it to where they would mess up? Do you think He wanted them to fall? Five minutes into studying the nature of God and you know that God does not tempt anyone to sin (James 1:13). That means He had to have another plan set up.

Do you remember how "Plan A" was for the Jews to accept Jesus as their Messiah the first time around? The Church Age, how it is today, was "Plan B." "Plan A," when it came to creation, was for there to be sinless human beings multiplying on the Earth glorifying God for all eternity. What we're experiencing now is "Plan B."

And so, like all good stories end, God's story ends right where it started: with sinless human beings living on Earth and making more sinless human beings to give Him glory.

Ps. 10:16, "The <u>LORD is King for ever and ever</u>: the heathen are perished out of his land."

Is. 9:6-7, "For unto us a child is born, unto us a son is given: and the government shall be upon his shoulder: and his name shall be called Wonderful, Counsellor, The mighty God, The everlasting Father, The Prince of Peace. <u>Of the increase of his government and peace there shall be no end</u>, upon the throne of David, and upon his kingdom, to order it, and to establish it with judgment and with justice from henceforth even for ever. The zeal of the LORD of hosts will perform this."

In the Isaiah verses, the thing that has *"no end"* is the *"increase"* of Christ's kingdom. It doesn't get any simpler than that: His kingdom does not stop increasing. It wouldn't take long for perfect people who never die to fill the Earth with perfect people who will never die. What happens then? Well, there's the entire universe, the *new* universe that is *not cursed*, and has not yet been created. Once the Earth is filled, these sinless beings go to live on other inhabitable planets that are not cursed.

New Jerusalem will be the capital of the Earth, and it will be inhabited by saved Christians, born again into the spiritual body of Christ (Gal. 4:26). These people will not be married or given in marriage, and this applies to anyone that has been resurrected from any age (Matt. 22:30). These individuals will have glorified bodies, like the risen Christ does (I Cor. 15; I John 3:2). They will be giving glory to God for all eternity, and possibly ruling and reigning with Him throughout all eternity (as they will in the Millennial Kingdom).

The Earth will be populated by the chiefest of nations, Israel. The Jew will have the Earth and own the land promised to him by God. Abraham's seed will be as the stars of Heaven and the sand which is upon the sea shore (Gen. 22:17). The resurrected Jews will be as the angels of God in Heaven, not given in marriage.

Everyone that will be a Jew on Earth will have been resurrected or raptured at some point, meaning they will not reproduce. At the end of the Tribulation, the entire surviving nation of Israel turns to the Lord Jesus Christ as their Messiah, and they are raptured in the post-Tribulation Rapture, giving them a resurrection body. Ironically, having been wiped out and despised by so many for being a "lesser race," they will be a rare and elite race throughout the universe. Imagine the honor of a Jew with a resurrection body among the eventual trillions and quadrillions of multiplying Gentiles throughout the universe.

The universe will be inhabited by the Gentiles. Resurrected Gentiles that are not part of the body of Christ (An example would be people before Abraham. Adam is one of these), will be as the angels of God in Heaven, not given in marriage. However, the surviving Gentiles from the Millennium will reproduce, and they're the only ones who do. They do not have resurrection bodies; they have bodies like Adam and Eve did in the garden.

There will be no death, no sin, no Devil, no old nature, and no influence from a "worldly" society. In the Everlasting Kingdom, "natural" people will eat from the Tree of Life and live forever sinlessly, like Adam was supposed to. There will be no possible form of temptation to the contrary; every individual will gladly and freely eat of the Tree of Life. Maybe God will make a tree of life for every planet. Maybe that was part of Plan A as well.

People will hear stories of what it was like to not see Christ, and yet follow Him - what it was like to serve Him by faith. They'll hear stories of what it was like to live on a sin-cursed Earth, and what it was like to be saved from a sinful life - to be changed, and to be given the power to overcome the world, the flesh, and the Devil. The stories will be told of people who gave their lives for Christ before political and religious tyrants, what it was like for a Jewish man, trying to stay faithful to God, hoping and praying for his Messiah to come, and what it was like for those who endured the wrath of the Antichrist, those who were tortured and beheaded.

Those born in the Everlasting Kingdom will praise God for all eternity for His goodness, love, and holiness, and that they'll not have to worry about sin and death. They'll praise Him forever for making a world and universe that is perfect for them to live in. They'll praise Him that they'll get to play a small part in God's amazing plan, and that they'll have the privilege of serving Him and praising Him for all eternity.

And so will we.

Even so, come, Lord Jesus.

The End

APPENDIX

CONSECUTIVE ORDER OF EVENTS

4004 B.C.:
Fall of Lucifer, Rev. 12:3-4

3 B.C.:
Baby Jesus Escapes Death, Rev. 12:1-5

29 A.D.:
Jesus is Caught Up to Heaven. Rev. 12:5

29 to 150 A.D.:
Ephesus Period, Rev. 1:1-2:7

150 to 325 A.D.:
Smyrna Period, Rev. 2:8-11

325 to 500 A.D:
Pergamos Period, Rev. 2:12-17

500 to 1000 A.D.:
Tyatira Period, Rev. 2:24-29

1000 to 1500 A.D.:
Sardis Period, Rev. 3:1-6

1500 to 1900 A.D.:
Philadelphia Period, Rev. 3:7-13

1900 to 20?? A.D.:
Laodicea Period, Rev. 3:14-22

20?? A.D.:
Rapture of the Church, Rev. 4-5
Judgment Seat of Christ, I Cor. 3:11-15
First Year of Tribulation:
144,000 Sealed, Rev. 7
Signing of the Covenant, Dan. 9:27
First Seal, White Horse, Rev. 6:1-2
Second Seal, Red Horse, Rev. 6:3-4

Second Year of Tribulation:
Third Seal, Black Horse, Rev. 6:5-6
Disease and Earthquakes, Matt. 24:7
Russia and Allies Attack Israel, Ez. 38-39

Three Days before the Mid-Point:
Moses and Elijah Arrive on Earth, Rev. 11:1-6
Antichrist Assassinated, Rev. 13:3-4
War in Heaven, Rev. 12:7-12

Mid-Point:
Antichrist Resurrected, Rev. 13:3-4
Temple Desecration, Rev.13, II Thess. 2:3-4
Breaking of the Covenant, Dan. 9:27, Is. 28:28

Mid-Point to Fifth Year of Tribulation:
Mark of the Beast, Rev. 13
World Church Destroyed, Rev. 17
Israel Flees, Rev. 12:6;13-17, Matt. 24:16-21

Fourth Seal, Pale Horse, Rev. 6:7-8
Fifth Seal, Martyrs, Rev. 6:9-11
First Trumpet, Rev. 8:2-7
Second Trumpet, Rev. 8:8-9
Third Trumpet, Rev. 8:10-11
Fourth Trumpet, Rev. 8:12-13

Fifth Year to Fifth Year & Fifth Month:
Fifth Trumpet & First Woe, Rev. 9:1-12
Rapture of 144,000, Rev. 14:1-5, Matt. 25:1-13
First Angel, Everlasting Gospel, Rev. 14:6-7
Second Angel, Rev. 14:8
Third Angel, Rev. 14:9-14

Fifth Year & Fifth Month to Sixth Year & Six Month:
Sixth Trumpet, Rev. 9:13-21

Six Months from the Advent to Three Days from the Advent:
Antichrist's Power Struggles, Dan. 11:40-45
First Vial, Rev. 15:1-16:2
Second Vial, Rev. 16:3
Third Vial, Rev. 16:4-7
Fourth Vial, Rev. 16:8-9
Fifth Vial, Rev. 16:10-11
Sixth Vial, Rev. 16:12-16
Antichrist's Final Campaign, Rev. 16:13-16

Three Days from the Advent:
Half of Jerusalem is Captured, Zech. 14:2
Two Witnesses Beheaded, Rev. 11:7-10

Day of Second Advent:
Two Witnesses Raptured, Rev. 11:11-12
Great Earthquake, Rev. 11:13; 16:20
Second Woe, Rev. 11:14
Rome Destroyed, Rev. 16:19; 18
Great Hail, Rev. 16:21
Battle at Bozra, Is. 63:1-6
Post-Trib Rapture, Rev. 14:15-16, Mt. 24:29-31
Third Woe, Rev. 11:14
Sixth Seal, Rev. 6:12-17,
Armageddon, Rev. 14:17-20; 19
Seventh Vial, Rev. 16:17-21
Death of the Marked, Luke 17:37, Mk. 13:39-42
Beast and the False Prophet are
Cast into the Lake of Fire Rev. 19:20
Seventh Seal, Rev. 8:1, Zech. 2:10-13
Mighty Angel Speaks, Rev. 10,
Seventh Trumpet, Rev. 11:15-19

Seventy-Five Days before the Millennium:
The Judgment of the Nations, Matt. 25:31-46
Renovation of the Earth, Is. 35:1-2, Amos 9:13
Satan Cast into the Bottomless Pit, Rev. 20:1-3
The Establishment of the Kingdom, Rev. 20:4

The Millennium:
Christ Reigns for a 1,000 Years, Rev. 20:4- 6

Satan Released, Rev. 20:7-8
Battle of Gog and Magog, Rev. 20:9
Satan Cast into the Lake of Fire, Rev. 20:10

Everlasting Kingdom:
Great White Throne Judgment, Rev. 20:11-15
New Jerusalem Descends to Earth, Rev. 21
New Heaven and New Earth, Rev. 21-22

PSALM 72
A PSALM FOR SOLOMON

1. Give the king thy judgments, O God, and thy righteousness unto the king's son.

2. He shall judge thy people with righteousness, and thy poor with judgment.

3. The mountains shall bring peace to the people, and the little hills, by righteousness.

4. He shall judge the poor of the people, he shall save the children of the needy, and shall break in pieces the oppressor.

5. They shall fear thee as long as the sun and moon endure, throughout all generations.

6. He shall come down like rain upon the mown grass: as showers that water the earth.

7. In his days shall the righteous flourish; and abundance of peace so long as the moon endureth.

8. He shall have dominion also from sea to sea, and from the river unto the ends of the earth.

9. They that dwell in the wilderness shall bow before him; and his enemies shall lick the dust.

10. The kings of Tarshish and of the isles shall bring presents: the kings of Sheba and Seba shall offer gifts.

11. Yea, all kings shall fall down before him: all nations shall serve him.

12. For he shall deliver the needy when he crieth; the poor also, and him that hath no helper.

13. He shall spare the poor and needy, and shall save the souls of the needy.

14. He shall redeem their soul from deceit and violence: and precious shall their blood be in his sight.

15. And he shall live, and to him shall be given of the gold of Sheba: prayer also shall be made for him continually; and daily shall he be praised.

16. There shall be an handful of corn in the earth upon the top of the mountains; the fruit thereof shall shake like Lebanon: and they of the city shall flourish like grass of the earth.

17. His name shall endure for ever: his name shall be continued as long as the sun: and men shall be blessed in him: all nations shall call him blessed.

18. Blessed be the LORD God, the God of Israel, who only doeth wondrous things.

19. And blessed be his glorious name for ever: and let the whole earth be filled with his glory; Amen, and Amen.

20. The prayers of David the son of Jesse are ended.

MORE BY RICK SCHWORER

A SNEAK PEEK AT

Thy KINGDOM Come: The Promise of the King

A dramatized retelling of the story of the kingdom of heaven: a physical and earthly kingdom that by and large has been won and lost by physical and earthly warfare.

Available in paperback and KINDLE
daystarpublishing.com ~ amazon.com
truthandsong.com

Excerpt from
Thy KINGDOM Come: The Promise of the King

As they headed up the mount, Isaac tried to get his father's attention. Abraham's thousand-yard stare was stronger than ever now.

"Father?"

"I'm sorry. Yes son?"

"We have the fire and wood, but where is the lamb?"

Abraham stopped walking for a moment and faced his son. His eyes looked right through the boy.

"My son, God will provide himself a lamb for a burnt offering," Abraham said and then turned to proceed up the mount.

"Don't you mean that God will provide for us a lamb?"

Abraham kept right on walking, unaware of his son's reply or of his own prophetic statement.

At the top of the mountain, Abraham and his son began to build the altar.

"This one is going to be bigger than normal, son," Abraham said. "We need to make it long enough for about three lambs."

Isaac's confusion had reached its tipping point.

"What's going on? You've been acting strange this whole trip. Can you please tell me what is going on?"

Abraham could contain himself no longer and wept aloud. He fell to his knees in front of the boy and covered his face with his hands. The sound of the man's sobbing was carried by the afternoon air up to the third heaven where the fifth cherub stood before the throne of God.

"He's going to quit!" Satan said.

"Just like Enoch and Noah?" the LORD replied.

Isaac helped his father stand back up. "It's okay, Father."

"No it's not, son. It's not!"

Satan laughed as the host of heaven watched the battle continue.

"Son, God told me to kill you!" Abraham cried. "He told me to sacrifice you on this altar. I have to do this, my boy! I don't know why he told me to, but I know he did! God's promises are real, and he must be willing to raise you from the dead if needed – but you have to die first!"

To say Isaac was stunned would be an understatement.

Satan smiled and turned to face the throne. "If you'll excuse me, I think I'll go visit that young man for a moment."

Isaac stood staring off into the valley as his father tried to gather himself. On instinct alone, almost mindlessly, he began to pick up more stones for the altar.

Then the darts found a new victim. *He's really lost it now! God didn't tell him that! The heathen do human sacrifices, not believers!*

The young man's eyes turned from being glossed over to focusing on his father, as another dart struck him hard. *Look at him, he's an old man. You don't have to go along with this. It's not as though he can make you do it! No one is going to blame you if you stop this madness. Your father will thank you later.*

Isaac began to give in. "Father, I..."

That's it! Tell him he's crazy! Tell him you're going to start looking for a real lamb to kill, and that he needs to take a seat. Tell him!

"Father, I think you need to sit down."

"What, son?"

"It's been a long trip, Father. Please sit down and rest. I'll build the altar and then you can do what the LORD told you to do."

26769548R00123

Made in the USA
Charleston, SC
19 February 2014